PARENT PROGRAMS
& OPEN HOUSES

Thanks to my husband and children whose
love, support, and patience helped to make this
book possible.

PARENT PROGRAMS & OPEN HOUSES

By:
Susan Spaete

Art:
Rick Abbott
Bill Peck

A  Publication

ISBN 0-943452-08-2

COVER CONSULTANTS:
Pat and Greg Samata
Samata Associates, Inc.
Dundee, Illinois 60118

CREDITS:

Building Blocks has made every effort to trace the ownership of all copyrighted material and secure permission from copyright holders. Any errors or omissions are inadvertent, and the publisher will be pleased to make the necessary corrections in future printings. Many thanks to all of these authors and publishers.

Valerie Bielsker, ''All About Dinosaurs.'' Used by permission of MORE PIGGYBACK SONGS compiled by Jean Warren. Copyright, 1984, Warren Publishing House.

Tonja Evetts-Weimer, ''There Were Five In The Bed.'' Used by permission of FINGERPLAYS AND ACTION CHANTS, Volume II by Tonja Evetts-Weimer. Copyright, 1986, Pearce-Evetts Publishing Co. 241 Morrison Drive, Pittsburgh, PA. 15216.

Sylvia Knaack, ''This Is Jack-O.'' Used by permission of Sylvia Knaack.

Diane Van Vleet, ''Santa's Workshop.'' Used by permission of Diane Van Vleet.

''The Christmas Tree.'' Used by permission of INSIGHTS AND IDEAS, Board for Parish Services. The Lutheran Church-Missouri Synod.

''1 Is For the Manager.'' Used by permission of INSIGHTS AND IDEAS, Board for Parish Services. The Lutheran Church-Missouri Synod.

''Who Loves Baby Jesus.'' Used by permission of INSIGHTS AND IDEAS, Board for Parish Services. The Lutheran Church-Missouri Synod.

''What Do You Suppose'' Volume 1, No. 9. Used by permission of KIDSTUFF periodical, A Treasury of Eafly Childhood Enrichment Materials. Copyright, 1982, GuideLines Press.

''Grasshopper Green'' Volume 1, No. 9. Used by permission of KIDSTUFF periodical, A Treasury of Early Childhood Enrichment Materials. Copyright, 1982, GuideLines Press.

PUBLISHED BY:
BUILDING BLOCKS
38W567 Brindlewood
Elgin, Ilinois 60123

DISTRIBUTED BY:
GRYPHON HOUSE, Inc.
P.O. Box 275
Mt. Rainier, Maryland 20712

ISBN 0-943452-08-2
$9.95

Dedicated to

. . . those times when we share an in-school experience with our families and friends.

CONTENTS

YEAR 'ROUND PROGRAMS CONTINUED

END-OF-THE-YEAR PROGRAMS

●   ●   ●

INTRODUCTION

Creating a feeling of goodwill between home and school is an important part of every teacher's job. **Parent Programs and Open Houses** was developed to help teachers plan, prepare, and present a wide variety of gatherings which are child-centered, easy to manage, and enjoyable. This book is divided into four types of programs:

Pre-registration meetings.
Open house gatherings.
Year-round presentations.
End of the year get-togethers.

Planning Your Program

Programs with young children are fun! They are enjoyed by parents, relatives, and friends as well as by teachers and children. The key to any program is planning. Below are ten guidelines to help ensure a successful program.

1. **Schedule your program as an outgrowth of classroom activities.**

    The program should develop from what the children are doing or have done in the classroom. When this is done, the program will be a natural conclusion to a unit or classroom activity.

    During the week before the program review the activities, songs, dances, and rhymes in the order in which they will be presented, so that the children will be familiar with the sequence. One overall practice should be enough. Remember there should be no pressure on performance.

2. **Take turns being the narrator.**

    Give different teachers, and maybe parents who would like, the opportunity to be the narrator in the various programs. This way you can spread the responsibility among several people rather than always having the same person.

3. **Provide babysitting.**

    Set up a babysitting service for the very young children in one of the nearby classrooms or other available rooms. You might ask junior high and/or high school family members to supervise. This will free-up all of the parents and staff to enjoy the program.

9

4. Follow your usual routine as much as possible.

If the program is scheduled to occur during your normal school hours try to follow your regular routine until the program begins. The routine will help keep the children calm. If the program is in the evening or on a non-school day, have the children meet in the classroom before the program. Plan a few familiar activities for them to do.

5. Include the children in the planning and preparation.

The teacher should choose a theme for each program but the children should take part in the planning. The children can suggest favorite songs, rhymes, dances, and games. They should decide what part they will play so that the event becomes truly their own and they can participate as they want.

The children can make decorations, prepare refreshments, cut the nametags, and so on. By including them in so much of the pre-program planning, the actual program is familiar and relaxing.

6. Keep it short.

Young children should not be expected to sit through and participate in a long presentation. Fifteen to thirty minutes depending on the group is adequate. The program itself can be expanded in many ways, such as by providing displays for the adults to view before the children enter, by showing a short film, by providing refreshments after the program, or by having a potluck supper.

7. Keep it simple.

The best program will include songs, fingerplays, dances, games, and activities that the children already know and are comfortable doing. Avoid introducing new material just for the program.

If costumes are necessary they should be kept very simple. Children can make them in school or parents can help at home using instructions provided by the teacher.

8. Provide variety.

Programs are as much for the children as they are for the parents. Children need activity as well as quiet times. When planning the program, provide opportunity for both movement and rest.

If the audience is going to participate in the songs, rhymes, or activities remember to furnish the words and directions.

9. Consider individual differences.

Look carefully at your group of children as a whole. All groups seem to have a personality of their own. A precocious group might enjoy a dramatization while a quiet group may feel more comfortable with a movement or an "all-together" type of program.

Look also at the individuals in your group. A quiet child may be your prop person, hold a sign, etc. The very young child may benefit from sitting with his parents and coming up with them to perform with the group. Some children may be prepared to lead or do an individual part in the program. Consider all of your individual differences while planning the content of the program.

10. Accept the children's performance.

The charm of a program performed by young children is the children themselves. Even when the program does not go as planned, it will be a hit in the loving eyes of the audience.

Parents are very understanding of their children's abilities. If something happens, explain to the parents what it is and go on with the program. If a child decides not to participate, either skip his part or have an adult take it without drawing unnecessary attention to the child.

11

Organizing Your Children's Presentations

Each children's presentation is divided into three parts: the Program Booklet, the Planning and Preparation, and the Presentation.

• The program booklet begins with the children decorating the program covers several days before the presentation. When the covers are finished, the teacher can insert the agenda and add a class list.

• The preparation part encourages the children to get actively involved in planning and preparing for the program. The ideas are meant to help you get started. We encourage you to add some of your children's favorite activities to those suggested in the book.

Once you and the children have planned, let the children make the decorations, simple costumes, nametags, and refreshments. Enjoy reviewing the rhymes, games, songs, and dances you've chosen to present. Remember, half of the fun of a program is the planning and preparation.

• The presentation part is the complete sequence of events for each program. It includes the children's entrance, the welcome by a teacher, the narrator's part to help transition the children from one activity to the next, all of the words to the rhymes and songs, and special directions to help the program go smoothly.

Invitations

Several weeks before each program, have the children make invitations to take home.

To make them each child should cut out a large appropriate shape from construction paper such as a pumpkin for the Halloween Fun Fest, a dinosaur for Dinosaur Doings, or a teddy bear for Teddy Bears' Picnic. Using different art media let the children decorate their invitations.

Type and duplicate the information each family needs to know about the program. Give each child his copy of the information and have him glue it to the back of the invitation.

After school he should take his invitation home and give it to his parents.

13

Join Our Halloween ← Front

Fe   al

Back →

INVITATION

Event _____
Day _____
Time _____
Place _____
Guests_____
Special Considerations:
    Costumes _____
    Food _____
    Props _____
Reply _____
How many are coming_____

Back →

INVITATION

Event _____
Day _____
Time _____
Place _____
Guests _____
Special Considerations: _____
Costumes _____
Food _____
Props _____

Reply _____
How many are coming _____

← Front

15

PRE-REGISTRATION PROGRAMS

To help minimize difficulties children might have adjusting to a new school, it is important that they see their classroom and meet their teacher before the first day. If this is done they feel more confident and have a better chance of adjusting to their surroundings. This may be done in several different ways:

1) The parents may bring the children to the classroom while the teacher is working before school begins. Parents should be given a list of available times and appointments should be made so everyone does not come at the same time. When they arrive they can casually walk around the room and talk with the teacher.

2) Choose a week or so when school is in session to invite new children and their parents to come, observe, and/or participate with the children who are currently in the classroom. Send an invitation to these families informing them of the day and time you've scheduled for the visit.

3) Have a special pre-registration day when all of an enrolled class and their parents are invited to attend a shortened 'school day' session. (If the class is young or large you may want to divide the group into sections.) Parents may stay in the class to observe all of the session or split their time by spending part with the class and part in an informative session with a school representative who explains the workings of the school.

SPECIAL PRE-REGISTRATION DAY

Choose a special theme for the day to help coordinate your circle times, free choice activities, snack, and story.

The day will begin with the children's arrivals. It is important that the teacher is there to greet the parents and children as they arrive. Nametags should be given to both adults and children. Encourage each parent to help his child get involved by using a small muscle toy, walking around the room with him, sitting with him when he chooses an activity, or observing as he explores on his own.

When all of the children have arrived, the teacher invites them to circle time. Each child should be given the choice to have his parent accompany him to a mat, to stay with the parent and observe, or to go by himself. Circle time can consist of a variety of activities such as:

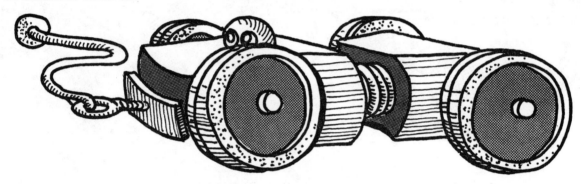

1) Get Acquainted — Let a puppet help you to teach the children a get acquainted song to the tune of 'Where Is Thumpkin?'

    TEACHER: *"Where is (child's name)? Where is (child's name)?"*

    CHILD: *"Here I am! Here I am!"*

    TEACHER: *"How are you today, (child's name)? How are you today, (child's name)?"*

    CHILD: *"I am _____. I am _____."*
    (This song is repeated for each child.)

2) Sing Simple Songs — Here are several examples:

RAGS

I have a dog and his name is Rags,
He ate so much that his tummy sags.
His ears flip-flop, (Hands on head and move)
And his tail wig-wags, (Hands behind back and move)
And when he walks he zig-zags. (Hands in front zig-zag)
Flip-flop, wiggle-waggle, zig-zag
Flip-flop, wiggle-waggle, zig-zag!

IF YOU'RE HAPPY AND YOU KNOW IT

If you're happy and you know it, clap your hands.
If you're happy and you know it, clap your hands.
If you're happy and you know it,
Then your face will really show it,
If you're happy and you know it, clap your hands.

If you're happy and you know it, stomp your feet.

If you're happy and you know it, nod your head.

If you're happy and you know it, jump up and down.

If you're happy and you know it, sit down.

3) Enjoy a Game — Learning games such as one called 'Colors' are fun. To play, the teacher gives each child six different colored objects to go along with the theme. (See below.) The teacher names and holds up a color. The children look at their objects and hold up the one that matches the color the teacher is holding.

4) Parents' Session — If the parents are going to join an informative session with another adult, the children should be told that after circle time their parents will be going to another room to talk to a different teacher about things that adults can do for the school. When they are finished, they will be back to share snack.

5) Explain free choice time — Explain to the children the different activities available to them in the classroom. Be clear about each learning center. Explain that when you give the clean-up signal, such as a song, everyone is to stop what they are doing and clean-up. During clean-up their moms/dads will come back and then they will have a snack.

6) A concluding song or activity — Form a circle and sing '**Child's Name** Came to School' (Tune of 'Farmer in the Dell')

CAME TO SCHOOL

Child's name *came to school,*
Child's name *came to school,*
Hi, ho the dairy-o,
Child's name *came to school.*

The child who is named goes into the middle of circle and the teacher names another child. Continue until all of the children have been named.)

After circle time, have the children move into the classroom and the parents (if planned) go to another room. Allow the children freedom to explore the activities around the room. When activity time is over and the adults have returned, give the clean-up signal. Allow time for cleaning-up with adult help. Show the children where snack is served and invite the parents to join the children. Snack may be cheese and crackers, finger gelatin, etc. along with a glass of juice.

When snack is over, parents and children return to the circle time area for a short story. After the story, chant a 'Good-bye' song and the children and parents may leave. Remind the children to take all of their projects home and that you are looking forward to seeing them soon. (Tell the children when they will return.)

GOOD-BYE TO YOU

> Good-bye, good-bye to you and you and you
> (Point to children)
> Good-bye, good-bye it was nice to play with you.
> (Have children point to each other.)

Picking a theme for pre-registration helps to determine name tags, color game aids, learning center activities, snack and story. A few examples are included here. The circle time activities, except for the 'color' game would remain the same for all of the themes.

THEME: Humpty-Dumpty

- Nametags: Humpty-Dumpty shape

- Color game for circle time: Give the children different colored plastic eggs. Cut matching egg shapes from colored construction paper for you to hold up as you name the color.

- Activities for free choice time:

ART — Make Humpty-Dumptys by gluing eyes, nose, and mouth shapes to an oval. Fold 4 narrow strips of paper like an accordion to make the legs and arms. Attach them to your oval shape.

BLOCKBUILDING — Encourage the children to build a wall, sit on it, say the Humpty-Dumpty rhyme, and fall off.

HOUSEKEEPING — Make playdough eggs.

SNACK — Humpty-Dumpty Crackers

Humpty-Dumpty Crackers

You'll Need:
Cheese slices
Oval Crackers

To Make: Using oval cookie cutters, cut cheese into egg shapes. Put the cheese on the oval crackers. Serve with Juice.

- Story for the concluding circle time: *The Golden Egg Book* by Margaret Wise Brown.

20

THEME: Gingerbread Kids

• Nametags: Gingerbread shapes

• Color game for circle time: Cut large gingerbread shapes out of different colors of construction paper for you and smaller ones out of matching colors to pass out to the children.

• Activities for free choice time:

ART — Precut a large gingerbread shape and let the children add features. Have the children glue buttons, paper cut like ric-rac, and other collage materials to the shape. Hang it on the school door when finished. Save it to use as a room decoration when the children return for the beginning of their session.

BLOCKBUILDING — Build a large house for the gingerbread kid.

HOUSEKEEPING — Make playdough gingerbread shapes and pretend to bake them. You'll need soft dough, a rolling pin, and several cookie cutters.

SNACK — Gingerbread Cookies and Milk

• Story — *The Little Gingerbread Boy* retold by Paul Galdone. Use felt board characters to go along with the story.

THEME: Shapes

• Nametags: Different shapes

• Color game for circle time: Cut a large red triangle, square, circle, and rectangle for yourself and smaller sets of red shapes to pass to the children.

• Activities for free choice time:

ART — Have the children cut different shapes and glue them onto plain paper. (Alternative: Pre-cut the shapes and have the children glue them to the paper.)

BLOCKBUILDING — Build with the block shapes. As the children are building, talk about the different shapes they are using.

HOUSEKEEPING — Have soft dough, rolling pins, and shape cookie cutters available. Talk with the children as they are cutting shapes and rolling dough.

SNACK — Triangle Sandwiches and Juice.

Triangle Sandwiches

You'll Need:
Bread slices
Cheese squares
Olives or pickles

To Make: Cut the bread and cheese diagonally in half to form triangles. Place the cheese on the bread. Cut the olives or pickles in circles and place on the sandwiches.

• Story — Read a simple shape book such as *It Looks Like Spilt Milk*, by Charles G. Shaw.

OPEN HOUSE PROGRAMS

The teacher plans open house programs to help acquaint adults with the school. These programs create a feeling of cooperation between adults and the children in their learning environment. They allow the adults to see what the children are doing and to communicate with the teachers. An open house is not a parent conference. It is a time when the school is open to adults. Some open house programs are planned for adults only and others involve the child coming with the adult. Included here are ideas for both types.

PARENTS' NIGHT

Several weeks before the Parents' Night send a letter to all of the parents informing them of the date, time, and place for the open house.

Nametags: Blue, yellow, orange, purple, green, white, pink, red, and brown circles.

Set-Up:

- Arrange the classroom, as if the children were coming, with the bulletin boards and room decorations in place.

- Place the 'Explanation Posters' on the appropriate tables.

- Arrange each learning center as described in the 'On Display' section for each area.

Refreshments: Juice, Coffee, and Trail Mix

INTRODUCTION

Introduce yourself and the staff who will be working with the children in the classroom during the year.

Have the parents think about what they remember most of their childhood, particularly of when they were their child's age. Was it a special friend, place, toy? Have them share their thoughts with someone sitting near them. Now, have them think of what they as a parent want their child to remember about this age. Parents and teachers help create memories the children will take with them for the rest of their lives. Everyone needs to work together to make pleasant, enjoyable memories.

"Tonight we will explain what happens in the preschool environment, why it is set up the way it is, and then give you a chance to work in each area."

Children learn through directed activity

"Each day of preschool has a circle time, a period during which the children sit together with the teacher for discussion, songs, fingerplays, language, large muscle, and directed math/science activities."

Children learn through play

"Each day a free choice time allows the children to choose what they would like to play from a variety of activities. Many of the activities are planned by the teacher to correlate with a topic or unit. They allow freedom of time, space, and movement. During this time art, dramatic play, science, large muscle, small muscle, blockbuilding, and cooking experiences are available for the children. This time also provides an opportunity to develop friendships and socialize with the other children."

Children learn through routine

"Your child follows a routine each day. (Discuss your particular time sequence for the session.) Children learn to clean-up and care for their personal needs. They are encouraged to take care of their own toileting, wash their hands before snacks, eat politely during snack and lunch times, and rest."

CLASSROOM ACTIVITY

"The classroom is divided into several learning areas, which we call 'Centers.' In each center tonight I have set up a display of materials as well as an explanation of the general purposes of that area. Your colored nametag corresponds with a color of the sign at one of the centers. The colors and centers are:

Art — Red
Housekeeping — Blue
Cooking — Brown
Blockbuilding — Yellow
Fine Motor — Orange
Music — Purple
Language Arts — Green
Science/Math — White
Gross Motor — Pink

Begin by going to the learning center which matches the color on your nametag. When I ring this bell, proceed to the learning center on your right until you have explored all of the areas."

Optional Activity: This type of Parents' Night may be expanded into two or three evenings by allowing more time at each center. Included with each learning center below is an optional activity. Use these if you're having an extended Parents' Night program.

Art Center

Red Explanation Poster:

1. Painting rules to remember:
   Wear a smock.
   Clean-up when you have finished.

2. We believe that the process of creating is more important than the product.

3. All creations are acceptable and worth positive comments.

4. It is important to experience a wide variety of media and methods such as painting, drawing, gluing, cutting, tearing, modeling, building, etc.

5. Teacher directed activities such as easy craft projects are periodically used to develop skills in cutting, pasting, and following directions.

On Display: Have a variety of art materials set up on a table near the easels. Include a box of collage items plus the different paints, chalks, doughs, and so on that the children use.

Optional Activity: Let the adults enjoy easel painting and pasting collage materials on pieces of wallpaper.

Housekeeping Center

Blue Explanation Poster:

Children enjoy dramatic play because:
1. It's fun.
2. They make friends.
3. It provides an opportunity to learn.
4. Children can try various roles.
5. They can release energy.

On Display: Have the daily props such as the furniture, cooking utensils, and pretend foods available for the parents to see. You might set the table for them.

Optional Activity: Have a 'prop box' filled with a mirror, hats, and different coats. Encourage the adults to try on different items and then look at themselves in the full length or hand mirrors.

Cooking Center

Brown Explanation Poster:

Cooking experiences provide opportunities to learn that:
1. There are different methods of food preparation.
2. There are proper ways to use cooking utensils.
3. Measuring and counting are necessary for accurate food preparation.
4. Some ingredients change when they are cooked.
5. Safety is important.
6. Sanitation, such as washing hands, helps prevent germs from spreading.
7. Nutritious foods help us grow.
8. Foods come from many sources.
9. Both men and women like to cook and eat.

On Display: Have five or six cookbooks which you use on the table. Encourage the adults to look through them and find recipes that they think their children like.

Optional Activity: Have all of the ingredients and the recipe on a chart for the parents to read while preparing the 'Trail Mix' snack they'll enjoy later.

Trail Mix

You'll Need: To Make: Mix all of the ingredients.
Peanuts
Sunflower seeds
Raisins
Cereals

Blockbuilding Center

Yellow Explanation Poster:

This is the area for:
1. Large motor development.
2. Dramatic play.
3. Learning about size, shape, and balance.
4. Socializing.
5. Sand/water play.
6. Carpentry.

On Display: Set up the variety of blocks you have available for the children to use. Put water in your water table and have the carpentry tools at the woodworking bench.

Optional Activity: Using the variety of blocks, have the parents erect a giant city. Add people, animals, and vehicles. Leave it up for the children to see the next day.

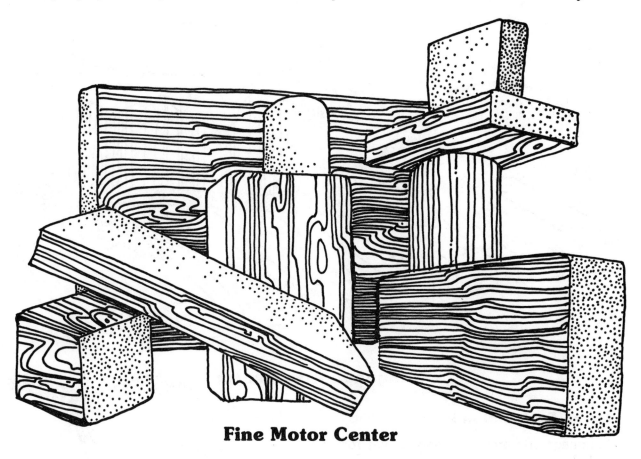

Fine Motor Center

Orange Explanation Poster:

In this area children:
1. Use their small muscles to develop eye-hand coordination and finger dexterity.
2. Develop thinking skills.
3. Develop social skills.

On Display: Choose a wide variety of manipulatives to set out on the table.

Optional Activity: Let the parents enjoy manipulating the puzzles, small blocks, lacing cards, and peg boards.

Music Center

Purple Explanation Poster:

The objectives of using music in an early childhood program are:
1. Appreciation.
2. Musical skills such as listening, performance (singing), rhythmic responses (clapping, rhythm, instruments), and creatvity (dance, words for a song).
3. Musical concepts such as high/low, up/down, fast/slow, loud/soft, even/uneven.

On Display: Lay all of the rhythm instruments on the table. Have your box of records sorted and available to flip through.

Optional Activity: Have the record player plugged in. Encourage parents to play songs from the different albums. You might also have the rhythm instruments out and let the parents keep beat with the instrument of their choice.

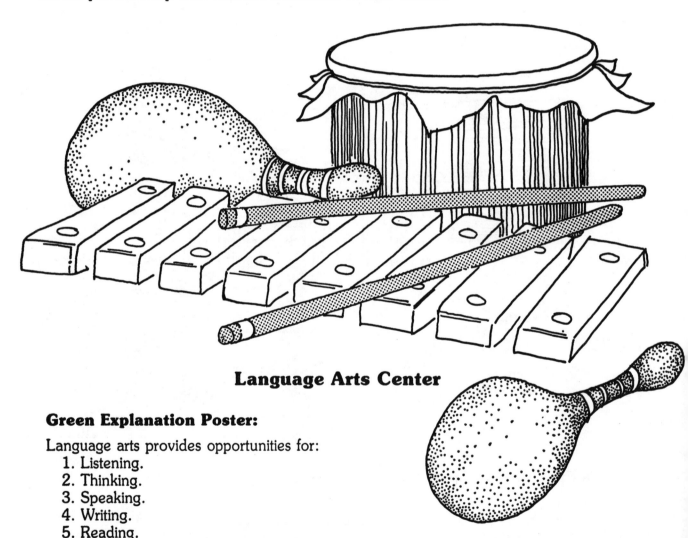

Language Arts Center

Green Explanation Poster:

Language arts provides opportunities for:
1. Listening.
2. Thinking.
3. Speaking.
4. Writing.
5. Reading.

On Display: Have the book shelf stocked with books the children enjoy. Open the language kits you use. Display the children's work.

Optional Activity: Show a filmstrip which you are currently playing for the children. Have the books you're reading to the children set out on a table.

Science/Math Center

White Explanation Poster:

Science opportunities are everywhere! What can you discover?

Math starts with the basics . . .
1. Measuring.
2. Sets.
3. Quantity.
4. Numbers.
5. Counting.
6. Shapes.
7. Size.
8. Positional relationships.

On Display: Have all of the math and science equipment, such as number puzzles, magnets, magnifying glasses, animals, etc. on the science table. If the children are collecting something such as leaves, have their collection on display also.

Optional Activity: Have several magnets and a box full of magnetic and non-magnetic objects. Have a posterboard divided in half, marked Magnetic/Non-Magnetic laying on the table. Direct the parents to pick an object, predict whether it is magnetic or not, test it, and lay it on the appropriate side.

Gross Motor Center

Pink Explanation Poster:

Gross motor activities help children to develop:
1. Basic skills such as walking, running, hopping, skipping, jumping, sliding, and galloping.
2. Body awareness.
3. Balance.
4. Positional relationships such as under, in, through, over, around, etc.
5. Ball skills.
6. Beanbag skills.
7. Rhythms.
8. Exercise.

On Display: If warm, set up this display outside. Have all of the riding vehicles in a 'parking lot' along with many of the other pieces of large muscle equipment that the children use.

Optional Activity: Set up a maze for the parents to maneuver around. Use such things as tires, the balance beam, and ropes.

Conclusion

Allow 5 to 7 minutes for each station. After everyone has had the opportunity to visit every center, call the group together. Give everyone a chance to get refreshments and then have a question and answer time.

FUN FEST

A Fun Fest is an indoor fair with games, activities, and refreshments designed for young children and their families. It can be an alternative to Halloween trick or treating. Planning should start in September. Possible organization can include a chairperson and seven committees: volunteers, tickets, prizes, booths, refreshments, clean-up, and games.

Tickets: Tickets may be sold at the door for 5 to 10 cents a ticket. Children take their tickets into the Fest and use one for each game they play. (The sale of tickets provides money for the prizes.)

Chairperson: Oversees all of the committees.

Volunteers: Volunteers are needed to monitor each booth for an hour at a time. For example if the Fest is from 4-6 or 5-7, volunteers would be contacted and scheduled in a particular area. A list of volunteers and times should be posted.

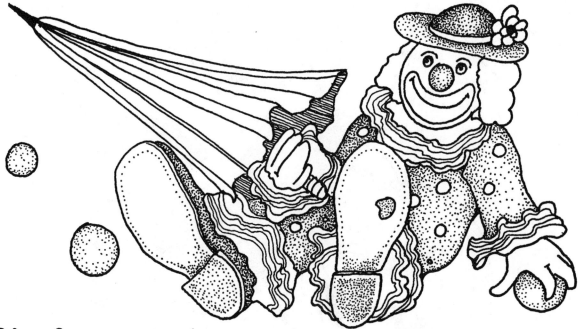

Prizes: Someone must purchase prizes such as small toys, pencils, stickers, rings, necklaces, etc. for each of the booths.

Booths: Booths are set up around the room for the games, refreshments, and art projects. Each person in charge of an activity may set up his own booth or all of the booths may be set up by a committee.

Refreshments: The refreshment booth may run on donations and used as a profit making opportunity to help pay for other activities. Food such as hot dogs, chips, candy bars, and cold drinks could be sold. Have tables and chairs for the families to use.

Clean-up: Have a large clean-up committee so the work can get done quickly and efficiently. Remember to have enough trash bags, brooms, etc.

Booth Suggestions

Art Booth: Set out the materials to make black spiders — scissors, glue, and an outline of a circle, 8-½″x6″ strips, and string for each spider. First the child should cut a round circle. Then add eight legs. The child can simply glue them so they hang down or he can fold them back and forth like an accordion. Attach a string at the top.

Fence Painting: Tape a long piece of butcher paper low on a wall. Have tempera paint in containers and a variety of brushes. Let the children paint a mural.

Duck Pond: Stick one of three different colored dots on the bottom of the plastic ducks. Put the ducks in a large tub of water. A child should reach into the pond, grab a duck, turn it over, and tell the booth attendant what color is on his duck. The color determines the prize.

Jack-O-Toss: Put a plastic Jack-O-Lantern three feet from a taped line. Give the child a beanbag. Have him stand on the line and toss the beanbag into the pumpkin. The child should continue to toss until he gets the beanbag into the Jack-O-Lantern.

Penny Pitch: Fill a children's swimming pool with water. Float several different size bowls in the water. Give each child five pennies to toss into the floating bowls. When he gets at least one in a bowl he can choose a prize.

Ring Toss: Stand a three foot pole in the booth. A child should throw rings (rubber sealing lids) around the pole.

32

Fishing Pond: Give each child a fishing pole. Help him drape a line over a screen. The booth attendant fastens a prize to the end of the line and the child fishes the prize out.

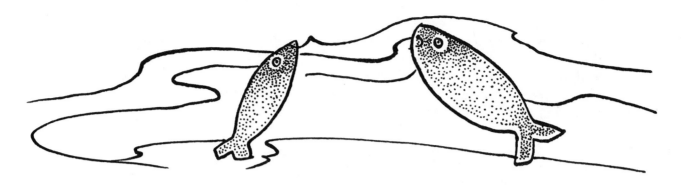

Lollipop Pumpkin: Color the bottoms of lollipop sticks with different colored markers. Poke the lollipops in a large pumpkin. A child should pull a lollipop out. The color of the stick determines the prize.

Beanbag Toss: Give each child four beanbags to toss at a target. When he hits the target he wins a prize.

Cake Walk: This game is similar to musical chairs and can be played with either chairs or large numbers painted or taped to the floor. The players stand around the numbers. When the music begins all of the players should walk around the numbers. When the music stops, a person picks a number out of a hat. The person on that number wins the cake. (Cake donations are necessary for this activity.)

Photo Booth: Draw large illustrations of characters, such as a dancer, princess, cowboy, and an animal on the four sides of a refrigerator box. Cut the box where the character's face should be. The child puts his head in the hole and booth attendant takes the child's picture with a Polaroid® camera.

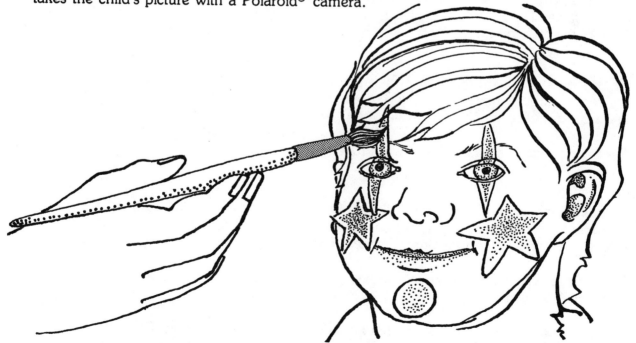

Face Painting: Using commercial face paint, have a person who is talented in art paint small pictures such as rainbows, glasses, names, snacks, etc. on children's faces.

SCHOOL DAY

This open house is designed for the parents and children to come for 1 to 1½ hours and take part in the regular activities that the children do daily. If the class is large it may be done in two sessions. Consider having one of the sessions in the early evening or on the week-end for the convenience of the parents who are unable to come during working hours. Using a lesson recently completed provides an opportunity for the children to show the parents what they have learned.

Set up the classroom as it is during the school day. Use the regular routine but shorten the duration of each activity. Encourage the parents and their children to stay together and do all of the activities. (Have a camera available to take photos to display afterwards.)

Circle Time: Parents and children should sit together. Have the children introduce their parents. The songs and activities should be familiar to the children. Repeat so the parents are able to join in.

Free Choice: Children can take their parents to the regular activities set up around the room. Enough materials should be provided so that both the children and adults are able to participate in the activities.

Clean-up: Parents and children work together to clean-up.

Snack: Snack may be made by children during class the day of the open house. For example have the children prepare cheese sandwiches and wrap them in plastic bags. Mix juice to drink. Keep the snack in the refrigerator.

Storytime: Children and parents should get comfortable together as a story is read or filmstrip viewed.

Active Game: You may need to have two circles. A game such as 'Duck, Duck, Goose' or 'Farmer in the Dell' would be appropriate.

Good-bye: Parents and children take all materials home.

GRANDPARENTS' DAY

What a treasure children have in their grandparents and older friends. What fun it is to share a day at school with them. This open house could take place during a unit on the 'Family.'

Invitations are sent home to the parents inviting an older friend or grandparent to school at a specific time. The children should arrive at the regular time, their guest may arrive ½ to 1 hour after them.

When their guests arrive, the children should find chairs for them. Provide adequate seating as it may be difficult for some to sit on mats or small chairs. If they arrive during a free choice time they are invited to either watch or join the children in the activities in which they are engaged.

Circle Time: After clean-up call the children together. Have each child introduce his guest. Children may sing their favorite songs and perform a few fingerplays. Then they should sit next to their guest and play the following game.

'Now/Long Ago' activity. The teacher tells the group that she will ask some questions. Each child and adult will have an opportunity to answer a question. Examples of questions for the teacher to ask:

1. CHILD: How do you go to the store?
   GUEST: How did you go when you were a child?

2. CHILD: How do you get to school?
   GUEST: How did you get to school when you were a child?

3. CHILD: What is your favorite thing to do when you are not at school?
   GUEST: What was you favorite childhood activity?

4. CHILD: What does your mother ask you to do for her?
   GUEST: What did your mother ask you to do as a child?

5. CHILD: What is your favorite treat?
   GUEST: What was your favorite treat?

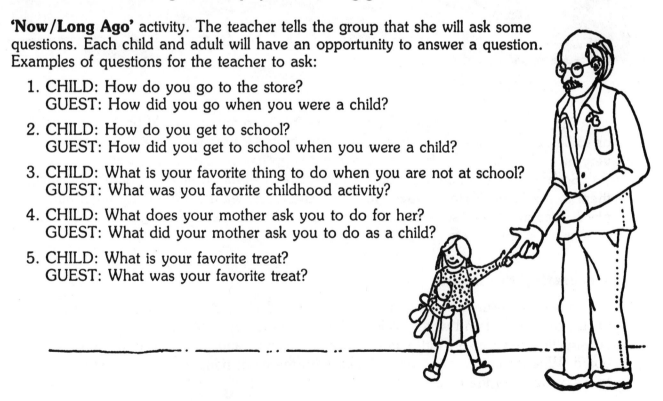

Snack Time: Guests are invited to join in snack. Prior to the guests' visit, the children will have made applesauce or muffins or cut bananas into chunks and put a toothpick in each one. Have this with juice.

Storytime: The children can sit with their guests as the teacher reads the story of *Little Bear's Visit* by Else Holmelund Minarik. (An option would be to ask one of the guests ahead of time to tell a story.)

Good-bye: The children present their guest with the art activity they did that day.

MAKE-A-HEART

This open house, designed for the entire family to enjoy, should be held a week or so before Valentine's Day. It is an opportunity for everyone to design and make his very own Valentine cards from materials and supplies available in the room.

Several weeks before the program send a letter home to all of the families inviting them to the Make-A-Heart Open House. In the letter, tell them the date, time, and place. Also include a list of any supplies you would like them to bring such as a pair of scissors, a smock, etc.

Decorating the Room:

Have the children make a giant Valentine card. To make it, fold a piece of pink posterboard in half and write "Welcome" on it. Have each child decorate a construction paper heart with various collage materials and then glue it to the large board. When everyone's individual heart is on the card, hang it on the classroom door to welcome all of the families.

Organizing the Room:

Have enough work tables available so that all of the guests have enough room to make their cards. Put a variety of supplies on each work table:

Scissors
Glue
Construction paper
Pencils
Stapler

On a special table in the center of the room lay out all of the additional supplies people might need:

Colored construction paper scraps
Pieces of fabric
Various sizes of doilies
Ric-rac
Old valentine cards
Valentine stickers and hearts
Macaroni noodles
Watercolor paints
Rubber valentine stamps and stamp pads
Various size heart shaped patterns made from posterboard
Yarn pieces
Crayons
Markers
Colored pencils

The people can go to this main table, get the supplies they want, take them to a work table, and assemble their cards.

Refreshments:

Have each family bring a red dessert or drink to share.

Extending the Open House:

If you want to expand this open house beyond simply making cards, begin it with a potluck supper for your families. Have each family bring its own tableware and a dish to pass. The school could furnish a variety of drinks. After everyone has enjoyed eating together, they can move over to the art area and begin making their cards.

37

YEAR 'ROUND PRESENTATIONS

HALLOWEEN COSTUME PARADE

Children Enter . . . . . . Parade Around the Room for Everyone to See
Teacher . . . . Welcome
Song . . . . *One Little, Two Little, Three Little Jack-O-Lanterns*
Fingerplay . . . . *Five Little Jack-O-Lanterns*
Dance . . . . *Now It's Halloween*
Song . . . . *This Is Halloween-O*
Fingerplay . . . . *This Is Jack-O*
Rhyme . . . . *Pumpkin Pie*
Refreshments

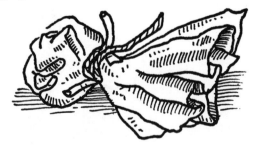

Program Covers — Decorate the covers with tissue ghosts. To make
them, lay the tissues flat, put cotton balls in the middle, bunch them to
form the heads, and tie strings around their necks. Add features with
black felt-tipped markers. Glue them to the covers.

PREPARATION

Children's Planning:

- The children will wear costumes they have brought from home. Discuss these and others that they have seen in stores.

- Let the children know that on the day they wear their costumes to school, they will have a costume parade. Maybe their parents, brothers, sisters, grandparents, or neighbors would like to come.

- Let the children suggest favorite Halloween songs and fingerplays that they would like to perform.

Classroom Preparation:

- Review the rhymes and songs the children have chosen.

- Have the children make construction or tissue paper jack-o-lanterns by forming hangers into circles and covering them with orange paper. The hooks of the hangers are the stems of the jack-o-lanterns. Glue black construction paper pieces to make the faces. On the backside of each jack-o-lantern write a number to coincide with the rhyme 'One Little, Two Little, Three Little Jack-O-Lanterns.'

- Have the children make jack-o-lantern stick puppets which have happy, sad, angry, or sleepy faces. They should cut out pumpkin shapes, use collage scraps to decorate the faces, and then glue tongue depressors or paint stir-sticks on the back. In addition, have several children simply glue orange scraps to white construction paper and attach a stick to the backside. They'll use these puppets with the rhyme, 'This Is Jack-O.'

Songs and Fingerplays:

- *One Little, Two Little, Three Little Jack-O-Lanterns*
- *Five Little Jack-O-Lanterns*
- *Now It's Halloween*
- *This Is Halloween-O*
- *This Is Jack-O*
- *Pumpkin Pie*

Costumes: Send a note home to the parents a week or more in advance letting them know of the program and plans for dressing in Halloween costumes. You might suggest to them that young children should not wear masks as they remove them almost immediately and that make-up is an acceptable alternative. You may wish to include a list of costume ideas as well.

41

Nametags: Black bats with names written in white crayon.

Decorations: If the program will take place in the classroom, things such as spiders made from pipe cleaners, jack-o-lanterns carved by the children, and black cats cut from construction paper would be appropriate. If the program will take place in another classroom, decorations are not necessary.

Set-up:

• Set the children's mats with their names on them in the presentation area.

• Lay their stick puppets on their mats.

Refreshments: Pumpkin Seeds, Pumpkin Sandwiches and Spiced Apple Cider.

Pumpkin Seeds

You'll Need:
Pumpkin seeds
Salt
3-4 Tbs butter

To Make: Save the seeds from your pumpkins. Rinse them. Add 2 tsp of salt to a bowl of water. Soak the seeds in water. Drain. Melt the butter. Mix the seeds in the melted butter. Spread them on a cookie sheet. Sprinkle a little salt on the seeds. Bake them at 250°. Stirring them every 15 minutes, bake for about an hour or until they are brown and crispy.

Pumpkin Sandwiches

You'll Need:
Bread
Cream cheese
Orange food coloring
Raisins
Chow mein noodles

To Make: Using biscuit cutters, cut the bread in circles. Mix cream cheese with orange food coloring. Spread the cheese on the bread. Add raisins and chow mein noodles to make features.

Spiced Apple Cider

You'll Need:
6 cups apple cider
1½ cups cranberry juice
¾ cup honey
2 tsp cinnamon
2 tsp allspice
1 tsp ground cloves
1 tsp ground nutmeg
Several thinly sliced oranges

To Make: Combine all ingredients and let simmer for about an hour. Enjoy the smells. Serve warm.

PRESENTATION

Children dressed in costumes enter holding the paper jack-o-lanterns they made at art. They slowly parade around the room so everyone can see their costumes. When the teacher shouts, "BOO!" all of the children parade to their mats and stand.

Teacher welcomes everyone to the costume parade.

NARRATOR: "The children have made jack-o-lanterns to go with their first rhyme, 'One Little, Two Little, Three Little Jack-O-Lanterns.' Watch as the children hold them up to greet you."

ONE LITTLE, TWO LITTLE, THREE LITTLE JACK-O-LANTERNS

One little, two little, three little jack-o-lanterns,
Four little, five little, six little jack-o-lanterns,
Seven little, eight little, nine little jack-o-lanterns,
All on Halloween.

Ten little, eleven little, twelve little jack-o-lanterns,
Thirteen little, fourteen little, fifteen little jack-o-lanterns,
Sixteen little, seventeen little, eighteen little jack-o-lanterns,
All on Halloween.

(After each child has held up his jack-o-lantern he will sit down. Now sing the song backwards and have the children stand up again. After the rhyme, each child should walk out into the audience and hand someone special his jack-o-lantern and then walk back and stand on his mat.)

NARRATOR: "The children have another jack-o-lantern rhyme they'd like to say. It's a little scary, so hold onto your seats."

FIVE LITTLE JACK-O-LANTERNS

Five little jack-o-lanterns sitting on a gate.
The first one said, "My, it's getting late."
The second one said, "Shh! I hear a noise!"
The third one said, "It's only some boys."
The fourth one said, "Come on let's run."
The fifth one said, "It's Halloween fun."
Pooooooof went the wind
Out went the light
Away ran the Jack-O-Lanterns on Halloween night.

(After the rhyme the children should form a circle.)

NARRATOR: "The children are forming a circle to dance 'Now It's Halloween.' The song for the dance is sung to the familiar tune of Hokey Pokey. Instead of using the different body parts the children are going to put themselves into the middle of the circle and shake."

NOW IT'S HALLOWEEN

Now it's Halloween, Halloween at last.
Now it's Halloween, we will scare you fast.
*We put a **bunny** in, we take **bunny** out*
*We give the **bunny** a shake, shake, shake*
And turn ourselves about.

(When a child's character is named he goes into the middle of the circle to do the 'shake, shake, shake.')

43

NARRATOR: "Halloween characters move in many different ways. Watch the children pretend they are the characters as they move around the room and sing the song, 'This is Halloween-O'."

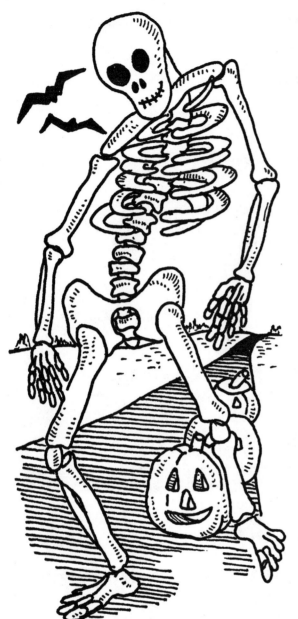

THIS IS HALLOWEEN-O

One little skeleton hopping up and down,
Hopping up and down, hopping up and down.
One little skeleton hopping up and down,
For this is Halloween-O.

Two little bats flying through the air,
Flying through the air, flying through the air.
Two little bats flying through the air,
For this is Halloween-O.

Three little pumpkins walking in a row,
Walking in a row, walking in a row.
Three little pumpkins walking in a row,
For this is Halloween-O.

Four little goblins skipping down the street,
Skipping down the street, skipping down the street.
Four little goblins skipping down the street,
For this is Halloween-O.

Five little children playing trick or treat,
Playing trick or treat, playing trick or treat.
Five little children playing trick or treat,
For this is Halloween-O.

(Children return to their mats.)

NARRATOR: "The children have made stick puppets to go along with the next rhyme. As they are saying their rhyme, watch for the different puppets." (Children hold up the stick puppets they made as they say the rhyme.)

THIS IS JACK-O

This is Jack-O-Happy (Happy face jack-o-lantern)
This is Jack-O-Sad (Sad face jack-o-lantern)
This is Jack-O-Sleepy (Sleepy face jack-o-lantern)
This is Jack-O-Mad (Mad face jack-o-lantern)
This is Jack-O-Cut-Up in pieces oh so small (Pieces)
But as pumpkin pie, he's really best of all.
(Children should all rub their tummies)

by Sylvia Knaack

NARRATOR: "Our last song has a surprise ending. Listen carefully and you'll discover what it is."

PUMPKIN PIE

My father bought a pumpkin
And much to my surprise,
We didn't carve a funny face
We made two pumpkin pies.
     by Dick Wilmes

NARRATOR: "Thank you for joining us for our costume parade. Please enjoy some Pumpkin Treats and a glass of Apple Cider."

THANKSGIVING HARVEST

Children Enter	Children Waddle in Like Turkeys
Teacher	Welcome
Fingerplay	*The Turkey*
Song	*Five Fat Turkeys*
Felt Board Story	Tom Turkey
Song	*Over the River*
Fingerplay	*Our Thanksgiving Table*
Rhyme	*Run Fast Little Turkey*
Rhyme	*Please Pass the Carrots*
Optional Prayer	*Family Prayer*
Refreshments	

Program Covers — Fold pieces of construction paper in half. On the covers have children make brown hand prints so that their thumbs become turkey heads and their fingers become feathers. When the prints are dry, the children can collage small scraps of construction paper to the feathers for color.

PREPARATION

Children's Planning:

- After telling the children that they're going to have guests for a Thanksgiving program, give them a choice of several snacks to serve.
- You may also like them to choose fingerplays and songs they know.

Classroom Preparation:

- Review the rhymes and songs the children have chosen.
- Let each child choose the artwork he would like to leave at school to decorate the room.
- If you are going to have a feast, have the children bring in the vegetables for the stew.

Songs and Fingerplays:

- *The Turkey*
- *Five Fat Turkeys*
- *Over the River*
- *Our Thanksgiving Table*
- *Run Fast Little Turkey*
- *Please Pass the Carrots*
- *Family Prayer*

Costumes: None

Nametags: Outlines of children's hands to form turkey shapes.

Decorations: Thanksgiving turkeys, dried corn, squash and vegetables in a cornucopia or basket of dried leaves.

Set-up:

- Place the children's mats on the floor.
- Make the felt characters for the story, 'Tom Turkey.' (If you do not use felt characters to tell the story, have the children make the characters out of construction paper.)
  - Solid brown, blue, yellow, white, green, red, orange, and purple turkeys.
  - Multi-colored tail for the brown turkey.
  - Blue bird, yellow chick, white lamb, green frog, red hen, duck with an orange bill, and dog with a purple collar.

Refreshments: Pumpkin Bread, Fresh Vegetable Tray, and Cranberry Juice.
(If you would like to expand this Thanksgiving Harvest into a Feast that everyone can enjoy, change the refreshments to Pilgrim Stew, a Salad, Pumpkin Bread, Dessert, and Milk.)

Pumpkin Bread

You'll Need:
½ cup vegetable oil
¾ cup honey
2 eggs
1 tsp molasses
2 cups of pumpkin
2 cups whole wheat flour
2 tsp baking soda
1 tsp ground cloves
1 tsp ground cinnamon
1 tsp salt
1 cup chopped nuts

To Make: Beat the eggs well. Blend in the oil and honey. Combine this mixture with the remaining ingredients. Grease a 5" x 9" pan and pour the batter into it. Bake at 350° for 45-60 minutes. Test it with a toothpick. Loosen the edges and let the bread cool on a wire rack.

From Come and Get It by Kathleen Baxter

Pilgrim Stew (Use if you're going to have a Feast)

You'll Need:
6 cups of water
Beef bone
1 onion
1-2 celery stalks
1-2 carrots
Tomatoes, canned or fresh
1-2 potatoes
Corn, canned or fresh
Any other vegetables the
   children would like

To Make: Ahead of time simmer the bone with the water to make broth. The children should wash, peel, and cut the vegetables into small pieces. (If an adult cuts them into sticks first, it is easier for the children to cut.) Add these and any other ingredients to the broth and simmer for about 45 minutes.

PRESENTATION

Children walk into the room while the song 'Over the River and Through the Woods' is playing in the background. The children go to their mats and stay standing.

Teacher welcomes everyone to the Thanksgiving Harvest.

NARRATOR: "The turkey is one of the main symbols used for Thanksgiving. He is a comical bird. The children have prepared two fingerplays for you."

THE TURKEY

Our turkey is a big fat bird
(Spread arms and hands in a big circle in front of you.)
Who gobbles when he talks.
His red chin's always drooping down.
(Dangle both hands under chin.)
He waddles when he walks.
(Hands on hips and shift weight from one foot to the other.)
His tail is like a spreading fan.
(Link thumbs together and spread fingers wide.)
And on Thanksgiving Day,
He sticks his tail high in the air.
(Keep same position and move fan over head.)
And whoosh he flies away!
(Unlock thumbs and bring arms in wide, fast arc to sides.)

FIVE FAT TURKEYS

Five fat turkeys are we,
We slept all night in a tree.
When the cook came around,
We couldn't be found,
So that's why we're here, you see!

NARRATOR: "The children will help tell you a story about another turkey whose name is Tom." (As the story is being told, the children should either stand in place holding their turkeys and characters or place them on the felt board.)

TOM TURKEY

(Elaborate on this story.) *Once upon a time there was a plain, brown turkey named, Tom. He did not like being brown. He wanted to be some flashy color instead. As he walked along the road, he saw a blue bird high up in a tree. He said, "Oh, blue is a lovely color to be. I wish I were blue." As soon as he said it, he turned blue. He was proud of his new blue feathers. He strutted along the road until he met a yellow chick. The chick said, "Whoever heard of a blue turkey. Why aren't you a pretty color like me?" Tom said "Yes, I wish I was yellow like you." And flash, he became yellow.* (Continue this storyline as Tom Turkey meets white lamb, green frog, red hen, duck with an orange bill, and dog with a purple collar. When he sees each of these animals he decides that is the color for him, but he finds himself unhappy. At last he wishes that he could be a brown turkey again with just a little of each color in his tail and his wish comes true.)

NARRATOR: "Thanksgiving is a happy time when families gather together. The next fingerplay talks about the 'Thanksgiving Table'."

OUR THANKSGIVING TABLE

Everyday when we eat our dinner
Our table is so small
Just room for mother, father, sister
Baby and me, that's all!
(Interlace fingers of each hand, pushing hands close together, palms down, two thumbs down for table legs.)

But when Thanksgiving comes and company
You'd scarce believe your eyes
That very self same table
Stretches out till it's this size.
(Expand table by pulling hands apart as far as possible keeping fingertips together.)

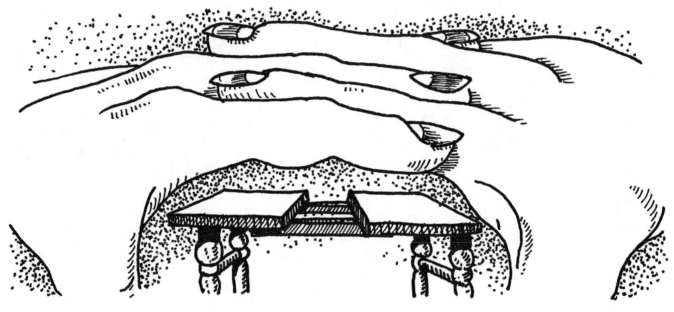

NARRATOR: "The first Thanksgiving was shared by the Pilgrims and the Indians. Today we will act out a rhyme for you showing you how one Pilgrim gathered food for the Feast."

RUN FAST LITTLE TURKEY

The brave little Pilgrim
Went out in the wood
Looking for a meal
That would taste really good.

First she picked cranberries
Out in the bog.
Then she saw a turkey
Hiding in a log.

Fun fast little turkey.
Run fast as you may.
Or you'll come to dinner
On Thanksgiving Day
        by Dick Wilmes

50

NARRATOR: "Many people have a big dinner at Thanksgiving. Listen as we tell you about it."

PLEASE PASS THE CARROTS

Pass the carrots
So orange and round.
Pass the potatoes
That grew in the ground.

Pass the corn
From stalks of green.
Pass the gravy
That's steaming in the tureen.

Pass the cranberries
I'll have a scoop of those.
Pass the breads
Made from rye and wheat doughs.

Pass the turkey
Oh! It's too late.
I can't have any turkey
There's no room on my plate.

by Dick Wilmes

NARRATOR: "In the next poem a grateful family shows what they do before they eat their Thanksgiving meal." (This is a great place to add traditions that people in your community observe.)

PRAYER

God is great
God is good
Let us thank Him for this food.
Amen.

NARRATOR: "Thank you for joining us. Please enjoy a piece of Pumpkin Bread, some Fresh Vegetables and a glass of Cranberry Juice with us." (Optional, you could have your Thanksgiving Feast.)

FESTIVAL OF LIGHTS

Children Enter ....Walking in holding candles
Teacher.......................Welcome
Song..........................*Hanukkah*
Felt Board Presentation ....Candle Counting
Game ....Spin the Dreidel
Dance ....Hora with adult participation
Special Guest
Refreshments

Program Cover — Make a Star of David for each program. To make each one cut two equilateral triangles that are the same size. Overlap them to form a star shape and glue them together. Glue the star onto the program.

PREPARATION

Children's Planning:

- Read the children the story of Hanukkah. After relating the events, talk with them about the Hanukkah celebration.

- Talk about how the children are going to celebrate Hanukkah in their homes. What traditions do they observe?

- Discuss the Hanukkah gifts they are going to give to their families.

Classroom Preparation

- Invite several adults to help you teach the children the Hora. Practice it several times. Form a circle and follow these directions:
    - Step with your right, kick with your left.
    - Next step with your left and kick with your right. (This may be all that you
    - would like to teach your children. If so repeat the steps until the music has stopped. If you want to include more steps, continue with the following.)
    - Put your right foot back behind your left.
    - Step with your left.
    - Step with your right.
    - Kick with the left.
    (Repeat from step 1.)

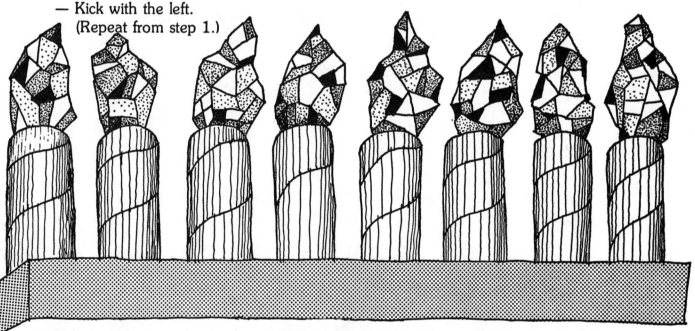

- Have the children construct a menorah. They can make the candles by covering one paper towel roll and eight toilet paper rolls with small pieces of tissue paper glued on with liquid starch. Have them use pieces of colored foil for flames. Insert the candles into a long, narrow piece of thick styrofoam.

- Using small milk cartons have the children make dreidels. They should cover their cartons with pieces of construction paper. Write the Hebrew letters on each side. Stick an unsharpened pencil or narrow dowel rod through the center.

- Cut seven or eight large star shapes. Have the children brush glue on them and sprinkle them with glitter. Let the first side dry, turn them over, and add glitter to the other side. Let them dry. Punch a hole in the top of each and attach a piece of cord.

- Have each child make a candle to carry while entering. To do this he should paint a paper towel roll any color he wishes.

Songs and Fingerplays:

- *Hanukkah*
- *Candle Counting*
- *Spin the Dreidel*

Costumes: None

Nametags: Star of David

Decorations:

- Hang the large Star of David shapes which the children decorated from the ceiling or along the wall.
- Place a real menorah or the one the children made on the refreshment table.

Set-Up:

- You'll need music for the Hora. You can use the song *'Hanukkah'* by Miss Jackie from her album *Sniggles, Squirrels, Chicken Pox.*
- Cut a felt menorah with the eight candles and shamash.
- Using masking tape mark the children's places for when they come in.
- Put the felt board in the center of the presentation area with the children's mats around it.
- Contact an adult to talk with everyone about the Hanukkah celebration.

Refreshments: Cheese stick candles, square dreidel shaped crackers, and milk.

CHEESE STICK CANDLES

You'll Need:
Assorted cheese pieces
Slivered almonds

To Make: Cut the cheese into long narrow sticks. Add slivered almonds for flames. Serve with crackers.

PRESENTATION

The children walk into the room holding the candles which they painted in class, go to their assigned places and stand.

The teacher thanks everyone for coming to share the Festival of Lights.

NARRATOR: "The children want to greet you with a special 'Happy Hanukkah' song.

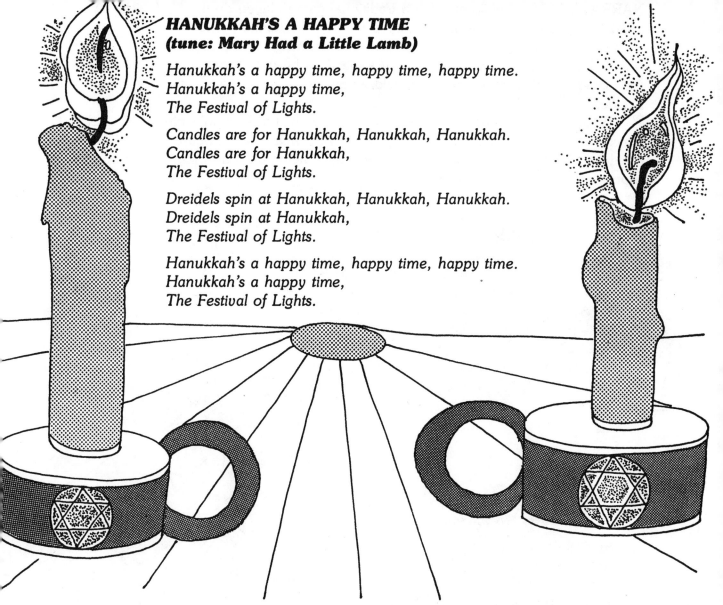

HANUKKAH'S A HAPPY TIME
(tune: Mary Had a Little Lamb)

Hanukkah's a happy time, happy time, happy time.
Hanukkah's a happy time,
The Festival of Lights.

Candles are for Hanukkah, Hanukkah, Hanukkah.
Candles are for Hanukkah,
The Festival of Lights.

Dreidels spin at Hanukkah, Hanukkah, Hanukkah.
Dreidels spin at Hanukkah,
The Festival of Lights.

Hanukkah's a happy time, happy time, happy time.
Hanukkah's a happy time,
The Festival of Lights.

NARRATOR: Hanukkah celebrates the miracle of how a small amount of oil was kept burning for eight days. In the felt board presentation the children will show you several traditions which surround this holiday. (Put the felt menorah on the board. Pass out the felt candles to the children.)

CANDLE COUNTING

The first candle is for the songs we sing.
(A child adds a candle for each line in the rhyme.)

The second one is for the gifts we bring.

The third candle is for the games we play.

The fourth candle is for a chance to pray.

The fifth candle reminds us of the latkes we eat.

The sixth is for the chocolate gelt which is a treat.

The seventh candle tells of the battles fought by Judah and the Macabees.

The eighth of the Temple and time to be free.

The ninth is the Shamash, the helper it's true, which lights up our room and our lives through and through.

55

NARRATOR: The dreidel game is a traditional game played during Hanukkah. A dreidel is a four-sided top that is marked with Hebrew letters. The letters are 'nun' which means the player gets nothing; 'heh' which means the player gets half the pot; 'shin' which means the player must put a piece in the pot; and 'gimmel' which means the player gets the whole pot. The children are going to play a variation of 'Spin the Dreidel.'

While the group sings the dreidel song, each child in turn will spin the dreidel which he has made (or a larger one set on a table near the felt board). When the dreidel stops the child will name the letter that is facing up, and then go around the room and look for a chocolate gelt prize.

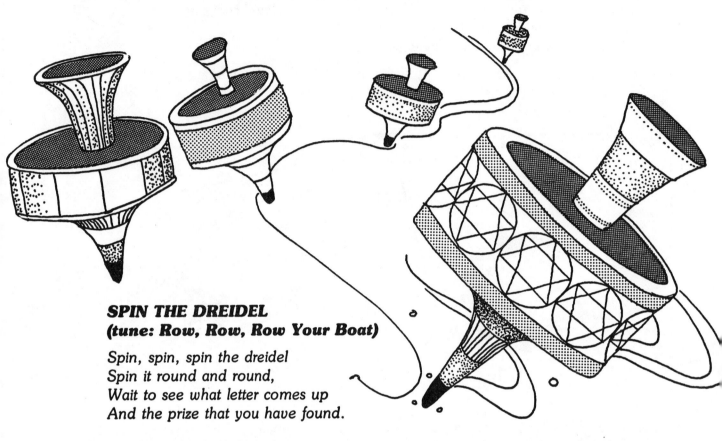

SPIN THE DREIDEL
(tune: Row, Row, Row Your Boat)

Spin, spin, spin the dreidel
Spin it round and round,
Wait to see what letter comes up
And the prize that you have found.

NARRATOR: "We would like to have you join us as we make a circle and dance to celebrate our festival today." (Form one or two circles alternating children and adults. Everyone hold hands. As the music begins the narrator voices the directions so all can hear.)

"Step with your right, kick with your left,
Next, step with your left and kick with your right."
(For a young group you may want to repeat these steps until the music stops. If your group is older you may want to include the next steps.)

"Put your right foot back behind your left.
Step with your left.
Step with your right.
Kick with the left."

Repeat from step one.

NARRATOR: Introduce your special guest.

NARRATOR: "The children would like you to join them for refreshments."

THE LITTLEST CHRISTMAS TREE

Children Enter . . . . Children Walk in to the Music, *'O Christmas Tree'*
Teacher . . . . Welcome
Fingerplay . . . . *I'm a Little Christmas Tree*
Song . . . . *Here's a Little Pine Tree*
Playlet . . . . The Littlest Christmas Tree
Song . . . . *Rudolph the Red Nose Reindeer*
Fingerplay . . . . *I Took a Lick of My Peppermint Stick*
Song . . . . *Up On the Housetop*
Fingerplay . . . . *The Christmas Tree*
Song . . . . *We Wish You a Merry Christmas*
Refreshments

Program Covers — Have the children cut triangle shapes out of a 3″ x 6″ pieces of green construction paper folded in half lengthwise. Next the children should use paper punches to make holes around the edges of the shapes. Then paste the trees onto colorful program covers such as heavy-weight wrapping paper, so the holes become the lights. Add trunks.

PREPARATION

Children's Planning:

- On several different days read the playlet, 'The Littlest Christmas Tree' to the children. After they are familiar with the story have each child decide which character he would like to be.

- Choose songs and fingerplays related to Christmas trees.

Classroom Preparation:

- Review the songs and fingerplays.

- Review the playlet. Decide whether the children should pantomime the parts or say the lines.

Songs and Fingerplays:

- *I'm A Little Christmas Tree*
- *Here's A Little Pine Tree*
- *Rudolph the Red Nose Reindeer*
- *I Took a Lick of My Peppermint Stick*
- *Up On the Housetop*
- *The Christmas Tree*
- *We Wish You a Merry Christmas*

Costumes: Costumes are optional. Here are suggestions, however, if you want the children to make them.

- Trees — Using large sheets of finger paint paper and pinking shears, have the children cut (or you pre-cut) triangle-shaped pine trees. All of the trees, except two, should be the same size. One should be larger and one smaller than the rest. Fingerpaint the trees with green fingerpaint.

- Bird — The child who is the bird should make a headband by cutting feathers out of construction paper and then gluing them to a cardboard strip. He can make his wings by cutting two pieces of 12" by 18" construction paper into large triangle shapes and attaching them to his clothing at the shoulders with safety pins.

- Father — The child who is the father wears a winter coat, hat, and gloves brought from home and carries a hatchet he has made from construction paper.

- Children — The children should dress in winter clothes brought from home.

Nametags: Christmas Trees

Decorations: Decorate a real or artificial Christmas tree with ornaments the children have made.

Set-up:

- You'll need a recording of the song 'O Christmas Tree' as background music for the children's entrance.

- Make felt board pieces for all of the children (tree, star, balls, tinsel, candy canes, presents) to accompany the rhyme, 'Here's Our Little Pine Tree.'

- Mark the floor with masking tape to show the children where to stand at the beginning of the play.

- Get a wagon or sled for the play.

Refreshments: A Christmas Tree Cake with Holiday Punch kept cold by a green ice ring.

Christmas Tree Cake

You'll Need:
4 eggs
¾ cup honey
1½ cups vegetable oil
1 cup white flour
1 cup whole wheat flour
2 tsp salt
2 tsp baking soda
2 tsp cinnamon
4 cups grated carrots

To Make: Beat the eggs, add the honey and oil and beat again. Add the dry ingredients, beat again. Fold in the carrots, and pour into a 9″ x 13″ well greased and floured pan.

Bake in 350° oven for about 40 minutes or until the cake springs back. Turn off the heat and leave the cake in the oven until it is nearly cooled.

Remove the cake from the pan. Cut it into a triangle shape. Use the extra pieces to form the trunk. Frost.

Frosting

7 Tbs softened butter
8 oz cream cheese
Honey

Blend the butter and the cream cheese. (Add a little green food coloring if you'd like.) Slowly drizzle a little honey over the mixture, stirring until it is a creamy consistency. Spread on a cooled cake.

Holiday Punch

You'll Need:
1 qt apple juice
2 qt cranberry juice
1½ cups fresh or frozen lemon juice
16 oz orange juice

To Make: Mix all of the juices. Chill and put in a punch bowl. **Ice Ring:** Fill the ring mold with green tinted water or lime juice. Leave ½ inch at the top. Freeze. Unmold and float in the punch.

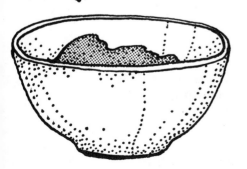

59

PRESENTATION

The children wearing their costumes walk in to the tune, 'O Christmas Tree' and go to their mats and stand.

The teacher wishes everyone a happy holiday and thanks them for coming.

NARRATOR: "The children would like to start by telling you about a little Christmas tree."

I'M A LITTLE CHRISTMAS TREE

I'm a Little Christmas Tree (Hands out at sides)
Glittering, glittering merrily (Twist body a little)
A star at my head (Point to star)
Gifts at my feet (Point to gifts)
And on all of my branches, candy canes sweet.
(Hands out to sides with big smiles)

NARRATOR: "It is so much fun to decorate trees. Watch and listen as the children sing and decorate their felt board tree." (Children sing, stopping at each line so those with felt pieces can put them on the tree.)

HERE'S OUR LITTLE PINE TREE
(Tune: I'm a Little Teapot)

Here's our little pine tree, tall and straight. (Add tree)
Let's get the ornaments so we can decorate.
First we want to put a star on top. (Add star)
Then we must be careful so the balls don't drop. (Add balls)
Hang on all the tinsel so shiny and bright. (Add tinsel)
Put on the canes, hook them just right. (Add candy canes)
Finally put some presents for you and me. (Add gifts)
And we'll be ready with our Christmas tree.

NARRATOR: "'Rudolph the Red Nose Reindeer' is a favorite Christmas character. The song not only tells a story, but has a catchy tune which makes it a favorite of many. Please join the children as they sing 'Rudolph the Red Nose Reindeer.'" (Everyone sings.)

Continue singing more holiday songs if the group would like. Here are some suggestions with which to begin:

Jingle Bells
Twinkle Twinkle Little Star
Silent Night
Up On the Housetop

You might want to take this opportunity to read the children the story of **Twas The Night Before Christmas.**

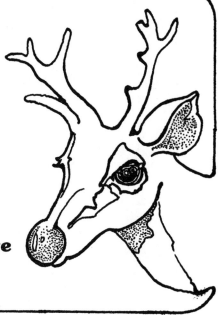

NARRATOR: "Bear with us now as we prepare for our play, 'The Littlest Christmas Tree'." (If costumes are used the children dress and get into their positions for the play. Another adult could help them if necessary. The narrator begins when the children are in place.)

Once upon a time, there was a forest of beautiful pine trees. In the middle of the forest were three pine trees, a large pine tree, a middle-sized pine tree and a little pine tree. (Trees bow as they are introduced.) One day it was very cold. The wind blew and blew. The trees shook with the cold air. (All of trees shake.) The trees were all very concerned. They were afraid that nobody would come to the forest for a Christmas tree when it was so cold.

Just then a little bird flew to the forest. It was very cold and was looking for a place to stay. It saw the big tree so straight and proud. It flew over to the big tree and landed on its branches.

The little bird said, "Please give me a home big tree. I am so cold and you look so warm and strong." When the big tree heard the little bird, it said, "No, I cannot give you a home. Christmas will soon be here and I must be ready when someone comes to make me into a beautiful Christmas tree."

The little bird was sad and was becoming colder. It saw the middle-sized tree with it's bushy branches and thought that it was so warm looking. It surely would allow the bird to stay.

The little bird asked, "Please, middle-sized tree, give me a home. It is getting colder and I must find a home tonight or I will freeze."

The middle-sized tree answered, "What, give you a home? You would ruin my beautiful bushy branches which are just the right size to handle delicate ornaments. No, No! Please go away."

By this time the little bird was very cold. The closest tree was a little tree with only a few branches. The bird flew towards the little tree and just made it to the branches.

The little bird asked, "Please little tree, I cannot find a home. May I warm myself in your branches?" The littlest tree felt sorry for the poor little bird. "Yes," it answered, "You may stay in my branches although they aren't very big. I hoped I would be a Christmas tree too, but I am too small and my branches are not straight or bushy."

The next morning a father and his children came into the woods. (Father carries his paper hatchet. Children pull sled or wagon.) They walked from tree to tree to find the right one. When they came to the big tree one of the children said, "Look at this big tree, should we cut this one?"

The father said, "No, it is much too big for our small room."

The other child ran to the middle-sized tree and said, "Here is a nice tree. It is not too big. Should we cut this tree?"

The father looked at the tree and said, "That tree looks as though it could hold many ornaments but we only have a few. I don't think it is right for us."

The children ran to the littlest tree and shouted, "This tree is not too big. It doesn't have too many branches, but there is a bird living in it. Can we cut this one for our Christmas tree?"

Father came to look at the little tree. He said, "Yes, this is the right tree for us. We can help the little bird stay warm by building him a house under the eaves while we decorate our little Christmas tree."

So they cut down the tree, (pantomime) put it in the sled, (tree sits in the wagon) and they carefully kept the little bird warm as they took it home for Christmas. (All of the children bow, then take off their costumes, set them aside and walk back to their mats.)

by Susan Spaete

NARRATOR: "I wonder if the littlest Christmas tree was decorated with candy canes? Listen to what happens to the candy canes on our Christmas tree."

I TOOK A LICK OF MY PEPPERMINT STICK

I took a lick of my peppermint stick, (Act out words)
And I thought it tasted yummy,
It used to hang on my Christmas tree,
But I like it better in my tummy.

NARRATOR: "Stockings, Santa, and toys, along with the tree make Christmas fun. The children will sing, 'Up On the Housetop,' a jolly Christmas song for you." (Children sing.)

UP ON THE HOUSETOP

Up on the housetop reindeer pause,
Out jumps dear old Santa Claus.
Down through the chimney with lots of toys,
All for the little ones, Christmas joys.
Ho, ho, ho! Who wouldn't go?
Ho, ho, ho! Who wouldn't go?
Up on the housetop, click, click, click.
Down through the chimney with good St. Nick.

NARRATOR: "The Christmas tree is said to be a German tradition decorated to celebrate the birth of Jesus. Our next poem tells us more about it."

THE CHRISTMAS TREE

See all the Christmas trees growing so high (Make triangle shape)
Pointing like church steeples up to the sky. (Point up)
Hear all the Christmas bells singing and ringing
(Point fingers down and move back and forth)
Join all God's children so merrily singing. (Frame face with hands)
Singing for Jesus asleep on the hay, (Rocking motion)
For Christmas, we know, is Jesus' birthday.
(Hold up finger and blow out candle)

     from Insights and Ideas

NARRATOR: "Please join the children as they sing, 'We Wish You a Merry Christmas'." (Children wave to the audience as they sing.)

WE WISH YOU A MERRY CHRISTMAS

We wish you a Merry Christmas,
We wish you a Merry Christmas,
We wish you a Merry Christmas,
And a Happy New Year!

NARRATOR: "Thank you for joining us for an evening of holiday cheer. The children have made a special dessert they would like to share with you. Thank you."

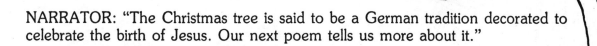

63

THE COLORS OF CHRISTMAS

Children Enter	Children Walk in Twirling Their Streamers
Teacher.	Welcome
Song	*S A N T A*
Fingerplay	*The Christmas Tree*
Song	*Twinkle, Twinkle Little Star*
Playlet	*Santa's Workshop*
Fingerplay	*I'm A Reindeer*
Song	*Silent Night*
Refreshments	

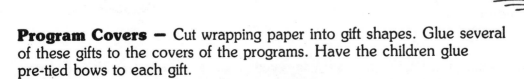

Program Covers — Cut wrapping paper into gift shapes. Glue several of these gifts to the covers of the programs. Have the children glue pre-tied bows to each gift.

PREPARATION

Children's Planning:

- Discuss Christmas with the children emphasizing the variety of colors associated with the holiday.

- Let each child choose his favorite Christmas color — red, green, yellow, brown, or white.

Classroom Preparation:

- Have the children make symbols to represent their favorite colors. Cut out large, simple outlines of Santas, Christmas trees, and stars. The children who chose red, green, and yellow can color or paint their props. The children who chose white can cut snowflakes and glue them to blue paper. Maybe they'll want to add glitter. The children who chose brown can make reindeer faces by cutting brown construction paper into triangle shapes and adding antlers, eyes, and noses.

- Review the rhymes and fingerplays.

Songs and Fingerplays:
- *S A N T A*
- *The Christmas Tree*
- *Twinkle, Twinkle Little Star*
- *Santa's Workshop*
- *I'm A Reindeer*
- *Silent Night*

Costumes: All of the children should cut purple elf hats to wear during the playlet, 'Santa's Workshop.' To make, cut crepe paper into 8″ by 20″ pieces. Fold the bottoms up for the rims, gather the tops, and tie them closed with different colors of yarn. Add bells if the children would like. Make one hat using red crepe paper with white yarn for Santa Claus.

Nametags: Christmas Trees

Decorations: Decorate a Christmas tree with ornaments the children have made.

Set-up:

- Lay the children's mats in the presentation area. Put their elf hats and 'color' props (Santas, trees, stars, reindeer faces, and snowflakes) on the mats.

- Cut ribbons or streamers in two foot long strips for the children to twirl when entering.

- Get a recording of 'Deck the Halls' to use while entering and 'Silent Night' to use at the closing.

- Get candy canes, train cards, lollipops, tops, dolls, and planes for the playlet, 'Santa's Workshop.' (Have them nearby to pass out as the narrator introduces the play.)

- Have a wagon for the playlet.

Refreshments: Reindeer Sandwiches with Christmas Punch.

Reindeer Sandwiches

You'll Need:
Slices of bread
Peanut butter
Stick pretzels
Raisins
Cherries

To Make: Cut the slices of bread diagonally in half. Spread each half with peanut butter.
  Add pretzel antlers, raisin eyes, and a cherry nose.

Christmas Punch

You'll Need:
2 qts apple juice
1 qt apricot nectar
1 qt lemonade
1 qt pineapple juice
1 qt orange juice
Cinnamon
Nutmeg

To Make: Combine all of the juices. Add cinnamon and nutmeg to taste. Put the punch in the refrigerator. Serve with red and green ice cubes.

66

PRESENTATION

Children walk in twirling their long ribbons or streamers and singing 'Deck the Halls.' (Collect the streamers and have the children sit down.)

Teacher welcomes everyone.

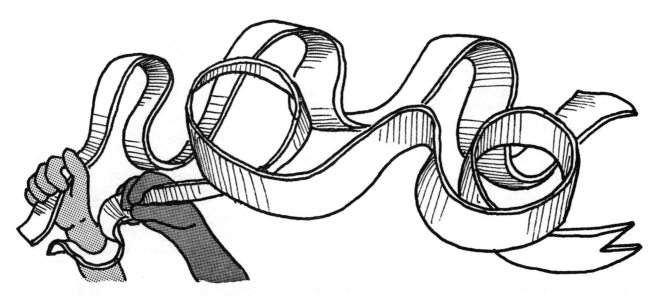

NARRATOR: "Christmas is such a colorful time of the year. We see red, green, yellow, purple, brown, and white almost everywhere. Today we will talk about our favorite colors and share them with you.

Red is the favorite of many. (The children who selected red as their favorite color should stand.) There are so many things at Christmas time that are red, but I think all will agree that the suit that Santa wears is probably the most famous red Christmas color. The children who chose red will hold up their large picture of Santa as everyone sings, S A N T A to the tune of B I N G O."

S A N T A

There is an elf at Christmas time and Santa is his name oh,
S-A-N-T-A, S-A-N-T-A, S-A-N-T-A and Santa is his name oh!

He wears a suit that's bright and red and Santa is his name oh,
(Repeat the chorus. Clap once instead of saying 'S.')

He has a beard that's long and white and Santa is his name oh,
(Repeat the chorus. Clap twice instead of saying the 'S-A.')

He brings us gifts on Christmas night and Santa is his name oh,
(Repeat the chorus. Clap 3 times instead of saying 'S-A-N.')

He fills the stockings in a row and Santa is his name oh,
(Repeat the chorus. Clap 4 times instead of saying 'S-A-N-T.')

Christmas cheer is what he spreads and Santa is his name oh,
(Repeat the chorus. Clap 5 times instead of saying 'S-A-N-T-A.')

NARRATOR: "Another favorite Christmas color is green. (Those who chose green should pick up the evergreen tree they decorated and walk over to the classroom tree.) Green is seen in nature. Our lovely evergreen tree is brought indoors. When it is decorated, it seems to say, 'Yes, Christmas isn't far away.' The children who chose green as their favorite color will stand around the evergreen as they enjoy the fingerplay, 'The Christmas Tree'." (The children should hold up their picture of the evergreen tree as they say the rhyme.)

THE CHRISTMAS TREE

I'm a little Christmas tree (Hands out at sides)
Glittering, glittering, merrily (Wiggle fingers)
A star at my head (Point to head)
Gifts at my feet (Point to feet)
And on all of my branches, candy canes sweet.
(Hands out at sides with big smile.)

NARRATOR: "When we think of Christmas we think of bright sparkly yellow. The tinsel and lights which we place on our tree make us think of the beautiful stars which adorn our skies. The children who chose this bright sparkly color will hold up their stars as we sing."

TWINKLE, TWINKLE, LITTLE STAR

Twinkle, twinkle, little star,
How I wonder where you are.
Up above the world so high,
Like a diamond in the sky.

NARRATOR: "Purple is a popular color these days. It is especially popular with the elves who are here with us today. These elves live in Santa's workshop. Let's see what they are doing today." (The children put on their purple hats. The child who is Santa puts on the Santa hat. The narrator should slowly read the poem as the children hold up the objects being described. More than one child can hold up the same object. Santa pantomimes the words as the narrator reads the last four lines.)

SANTA'S WORKSHOP

In Santa's workshop far away,
Many little elves work night and day.
These little elves make candy canes.
These little elves make electric trains.
These little elves make lollipops.
These little elves make wooden tops.
These little elves make dolls that cry.
These little elves make planes that fly.
Santa checks his list with a HO! HO! HO! (Santa unrolls his list)
And then he says, "It's time to go!"
Then Santa packs up his sleigh (Elves put toys in wagon)
And delivers the toys on Christmas Day!
      by Diane Van Vleet

NARRATOR: "Not all Christmas colors are bright and flashy. Some are plain colors, but belong to some very important Christmas symbols. Take brown for instance. What would Christmas be like without the animals which pull Santa's sleigh? The children who like brown will hold up the reindeer faces they made as they say our reindeer rhyme.

I'M A REINDEER

I'm a reindeer with antlers like so, (Hold hands over head)
Prancing and pawing and anxious to go. (Move feet)
I've waited a long time, I've waited a year,
I can't wait much longer, 'cause Christmas is here!

Around the world just one time a year, (Twirl around)
The jolly old elf and his eight little reindeer. (Hold up 8 fingers)
So many good kids waiting to find, (Look around)
The special surprise Santa's left behind.

by Dick Wilmes

(The teachers can pass a small gift to each child which they can open at refreshment time.)

NARRATOR: "Christmas has some very quiet and peaceful colors. The white snow falling from a dark blue sky makes us think of that first Christmas in Bethlehem. Please join the children as they hum the last song for the evening, 'Silent Night'." (Play a recording of 'Silent Night' as the children hold up their blue pictures with snowflakes.)

NARRATOR: "The children have prepared Reindeer Sandwiches and Punch for you. Please join them for a snack and have a Happy Holiday Season."

HAPPY BIRTHDAY, JESUS

Children Enter . . . . Children Walk in Swinging Their Bells
Teacher . . . . Welcome
Song . . . . *We Wish You a Merry Christmas*
Fingerplay . . . . *Mary's Secret*
Felt Board Presentation . . . . . . *One Is For the Manger*
Song . . . . *Away In the Manger*
Fingerplay . . . . *Who Loves Baby Jesus*
Song . . . . *Sing For Joy*
Reading . . . . List of Gifts That the Children Would Give
                                  to Jesus
Optional Reading . . . . Christmas Story or Filmstrip
Song . . . . *Happy Birthday, Jesus*
Refreshments

Program Covers — Cut stars out of construction paper. Brush them
with glue, lay them in a box, and sprinkle with glitter. Let dry and glue
them to the dark blue construction paper.

PREPARATION

Children's Planning:

- Discuss birthday parties with the children. Ask them, "What do you do at birthday parties?"

- Tell them that they are going to plan a party and celebrate Jesus' birthday at school. Begin by discussing who should come. What should we do? What should we eat? What type of decorations should we have at our party? What would you give Jesus if He were a baby in the manger today? (Write down the gifts they suggest on a large piece of posterboard. You'll use this during the program.)

Classroom Preparation:

- Review the songs and fingerplays.

- Decorate the room with the children's art.

- Have the children decorate Christmas bells to swing while entering the room.

- Sponge paint a large banner which reads, HAPPY BIRTHDAY, JESUS.

Songs and Fingerplays:

- *We Wish You a Merry Christmas*
- *Mary's Secret*
- *One Is For the Manger*
- *Away In the Manger*
- *Who Loves Baby Jesus*
- *Sing For Joy*
- *Happy Birthday, Jesus*

Costumes: None

Nametags: Cut birthday cake or balloon shapes from construction paper.

Decorations: Use birthday decorations such as balloons and streamers as well as Christmas decorations. You may also want to set up a Nativity Scene.

Set-up:

- Have a recording of Jingle Bells.

- Put the children's mats in the presentation area.

- Cut out the felt board characters (manger, Mary, Joseph, 3 wisemen, 2 shepherds, 5 farm animals, star) to coordinate with the rhyme, 'One Is For the Manger.' Have the felt board easily accessible.

- Hang the banner so that everyone can see it. If the children are going to hold up the banner, have it in a place which is easy to reach.

Refreshments: Birthday Cake and Holiday Punch

Birthday Cake

You'll Need:
3 qts popped popcorn
½ cup vegetable oil
¼ lb margarine
1 lb marshmallows
1 lb nuts (optional)
Red and green gumdrops,
   (optional)

To Make: Melt marshmallows, oil and margarine together in a saucepan. Pour over the popcorn which is in a large bowl. Stir in the nuts and gumdrops. Press into a buttered angel food cake pan. Cool and turn out onto a plate.

Holiday Punch

You'll Need:
1 qt cranberry juice
2 pts apple juice
1 qt orange juice
Juice of 2 lemons
2 qts water
¼ cup honey

To Make: Mix the juices and water. Dissolve the honey in a little hot water and add to juices.

   Chill the entire mixture for several hours to blend the flavors. Makes 30 servings.

PRESENTATION

Children swing their bells as they walk into the room and go to their mats. Play 'Jingle Bells' for background music.

The teacher welcomes everyone to the program and then invites the audience to join the children in singing the first verse of 'We Wish You a Merry Christmas.' Continue the song with these verses.

WE WISH YOU A MERRY CHRISTMAS

We wish you a Merry Christmas, we wish you a Merry Christmas,
We wish you a Merry Christmas and a Happy New Year.

Let's all do a little clapping, let's all do a little clapping,
Let's all do a little clapping, for Christmas is here!

Continue — Let's all do a little twirling, jumping, smiling.

NARRATOR: "Jesus' birthday was announced in many ways. The children will share some of them in this poem, 'Mary's Secret'."

MARY'S SECRET

Mary heard a secret. (Hold hand to ear)
The shepherds heard a song. (Hold hand to other ear)
The wisemen saw a star one night. (Point up)
And knew a King was born. (Put hands on head for a crown)

NARRATOR: "Next the children will do a felt board presentation that sets the stage for the first Christmas."

ONE IS FOR THE MANGER

One is for the manger, where Baby Jesus lay.
(Child brings felt manger forward and puts it in its place.)

Two is for Mary and Joseph, on that first Christmas Day.
(Two children come forward and put characters in place.)

Three is for the wisemen, who brought three gifts of love.
(Three children each carrying a wiseman come forward and put them on the felt board.)

Four is for the shepherds and angels' song above.
(Four children bring shepherds and angels to the felt board.)

Five is for the animals, who stood guard in the shed.
(Five children bring the animals to the felt board.)

As a Christmas star shown brightly overhead.
(A star is put over the scene.)

from Insights and Ideas

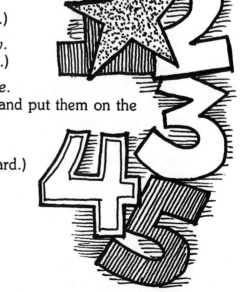

NARRATOR: "'Away In the Manger' is the first Christmas carol many people learn. It is a favorite of adults and children alike. The children will sing the first verse and invite you to join them in the second one."

AWAY IN THE MANGER

Away in the manger no crib for His bed.
The little Lord Jesus lay down His sweet head.
The stars in the sky, look down where He lay.
The little Lord Jesus, asleep on the hay.

The cattle are lowing, the Baby awakes.
But Little Lord Jesus, no crying He makes.
I love thee, Lord Jesus, look down from the sky,
And stay by my cradle 'til morning is nigh.

NARRATOR: "The love for this very special Baby is demonstrated in this next poem."

WHO LOVES BABY JESUS

Who loves baby Jesus?
Joseph loved Him. (Thumb)
Mary loved Him. (Pointer)
The shepherds loved Him. (Middle)
The wisemen loved Him. (Ring)
And I love Him. (Little finger)
Do you love Him? (Point to others)

from Insights and Ideas

NARRATOR: "Join us now in our next song, which tells the world of our joy in the birth of Jesus. It is sung to the familiar tune, 'Row, Row, Row Your Boat.' The children will teach you by singing the first verse and then you join them in the next verses."

SING FOR JOY

Sing, sing, sing for joy.
Sing out loud and clear.
Tell the message everywhere,
Jesus Christ is here.

(Continue — use clap, ring, shout, etc.)

NARRATOR: "While the children were planning Jesus' Birthday Party, they thought of many gifts they would like to give Him. As they were discussing the gifts the teacher wrote them down on this large piece of posterboard. I'd like to read them to you now. While I'm reading them, the children will be holding the banner which reads, 'Happy Birthday, Jesus'." (Have the children get the banner and hold it up while you read the list of presents written on the posterboard. After you've read the list, have an adult light the candle/s on the birthday cake. Remember safety.)

"We are going to dim the lights now and sing 'Happy Birthday' to Jesus while (adult's name) brings in the cake. Everyone please join us in singing, 'Happy Birthday'."

NARRATOR: "Thank you for coming. Please join us for Birthday Cake and Punch."

IT'S MUSIC TIME

Children Enter . . . . Children March in With Classroom Instruments
Teacher . . . . Welcome
Song . . . . *The Preschool Band*
Song . . . . *This Is the Way We Wash Our Clothes*
Song . . . . *The Wheels on the Bus*
Song . . . . *ABC Song*
Active Game . . . . Rhythmic Movement
Rhyme . . . . *The Body Band*
Song . . . . *Rock-A-Bye-Baby*
Special Guest
Refreshments

Program Covers — Precut different musical notes out of black
construction paper. Fold white construction paper in half and have the
children glue the notes all over the cover.

PREPARATION

Children's Planning:

- Talk with the children about different types of songs (noisy, work, travel, alphabet, movement, and quiet). Choose ones the children know which are appropriate for each category.

- Bring out the classroom rhythm instruments. Let the children try various ones and decide which type they would each like to make.

Classroom Preparation:

- Have the children make their own instruments to use while singing 'The Preschool Band.'

  STRUMMERS: Have the children stretch rubberbands around styrofoam meat containers.

  DRUMS: Cover coffee or oatmeal cans with paper and then decorate them with markers.

  SHAKERS: Fill juice cans with sand, beans, or stones. Reclose the containers and tape. Cover them with paper and decorate.

  BLOWERS: Cover the end of paper or styrofoam cups with waxed paper. Put rubberbands around the waxed paper to fasten. To play, the children should hum on the waxed paper end of the cup.

  RHYTHM STICKS: Cut dowel rods into one foot lengths. Have the children paint them different colors.

- Review the songs and fingerplays.

Songs and Fingerplays:

- Noisy Song — *The Preschool Band*
- Work Song — *This Is the Way We Wash Our Clothes*
- Travel Song — *The Wheels On the Bus*
- Alphabet Song — *ABC Song*
- Movement Song — *The Body Band*
- Quiet Song — *Rock-A-Bye-Baby*

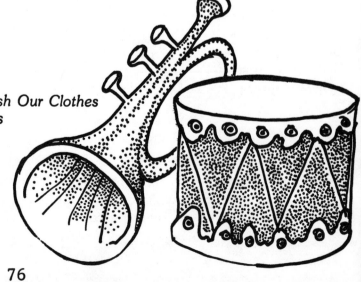

Costumes: None

Nametags: Drums or horns

Decorations:

- Have a display of real instruments which you have collected from the children's families.

- Before the program have the children create a large mural. Spread a long sheet of butcher paper on the floor. Let each child choose two crayons and sit around the paper. Play some fast-paced music and have the children dance with their arms, making a crayon design on the paper. Now play some slow music and let their arms dance again. When finished, label it, 'Arm Dancing.' Hang it on a long wall or bulletin board.

Set-up:

- Have mats with children's names on them placed in the presentation area. Put the instrument each child made on his mat.

- Have an empty box in which to collect the instruments.

- Contact a guest musician to sing, play an instrument, or lead a short sing-a-long. Maybe your local high school has a musical group which does guest performances.

Refreshments: Muffin Man Muffins, Shoo Fly Butter, and Milk

Muffin Man Muffins

You'll Need:
3 cups of bran-type cereal
1 cup flour
2 cups oatmeal
2½ tsp baking soda
½ tsp salt
2 beaten eggs
2 cups buttermilk
½ cup vegetable oil
1¼ cups honey
Raisins and dates

To Make: Mix all of the ingredients together. Fill muffin cups about ⅔ full. Bake at 400° for 20 minutes. Yield: 3-4 dozen.

Shoo Fly Butter

You'll Need:
Small carton whipping
   cream, room temperature
Quart jar with lid

To Make: Pour whipping cream into the jar and secure the lid. Let the children shake the jar vigorously until butter forms a ball at the bottom of the jar. Drain the liquid off; squeeze any excess liquid from the butter and discard. The butter is ready to use. You may want to add a little salt for flavor.

PRESENTATION

Children march in playing the classroom rhythm instruments. (After marching around the audience, they go to the front of the room, put their instruments in a box, and stand on their mats.)

Teacher welcomes everyone to an evening of music.

NARRATOR: "In school we have learned how important music is in our lives. Our music program emphasizes appreciation of music, listening skills, singing, rhythmic response, and creativity. Today we will begin our program using the instruments the children have made. We have instruments to strum (children demonstrate), instruments to blow (demonstrate), instruments to tap (demonstrate), and ones to shake (demonstrate). The children will play their instruments as they sing, 'The Preschool Band' for you. Listen as they name the different instruments and then play them."

THE PRESCHOOL BAND
(tune: Here We Go 'Round the Mulberry Bush)

The preschool band is coming to town,
Coming to town, coming to town,
The preschool band is coming to town,
Coming to town today.

The preschool band is blowing their horns,
Blowing their horns, blowing their horns,
The preschool band is blowing their horns,
Blowing their horns today.

The preschool band is strumming their boards . . .

The preschool band is tapping their sticks . . .

The preschool band is shaking their shakers . . .

The preschool band is going away,
Going away, going away,
The preschool band is going away,
Going away today!

(Have an adult or child collect the instruments and the children sit down.)

NARRATOR: "We have learned to enjoy singing. There are songs which help us get jobs done. Listen to all of the work we can do in one week. As the children sing, they will also show you how hard they work."

THIS IS THE WAY WE WASH OUR CLOTHES
(tune: Here We Go 'Round the Mulberry Bush)

This is the way we wash our clothes, wash our clothes,
Wash our clothes, this is the way we wash our clothes,
Early Monday morning. (Suit actions to words)

This is the way we iron our clothes, iron our clothes,
Iron our clothes, this is the way we iron our clothes,
Early Tuesday Morning. (Suit actions to words)

This is the way we sweep the floor, sweep the floor,
Sweep the floor, this is the way we sweep the floor,
Early Wednesday morning. (Suit actions to words)

This is the way we shake the rugs, shake the rugs,
Shake the rugs, this is the way we shake the rugs,
Early Thursday morning. (Suit actions to words)

This is the way we make the beds, make the beds,
Make the beds, this is the way we make the beds,
Early Friday morning. (Suit the actions to words)

This is the way we pick up our toys, pick up our toys,
Pick up our toys, this is the way we pick up our toys,
Early Saturday morning. (Suit actions to words)

This is the way we go to church, go to church,
Go to church, this is the way we go to church,
Early Sunday morning. (Suit action to words)

NARRATOR: "There are songs to pass the time while traveling. Today we are going to travel by bus. All aboard!"

THE WHEELS ON THE BUS

The wheels on the bus go 'round and 'round,
'Round and 'round, 'round and 'round.
The wheels on the bus go 'round and 'round,
All through the town. (Roll arms)

The driver on the bus says, "Move on back,
Move on back, move on back."
The driver on the bus says, "Move on back,"
All through the town. (Motion back with hand)

The wipers on the bus go swish, swish, swish,
Swish, swish, swish, swish, swish, swish.
The wipers on the bus go swish, swish, swish,
All through the town. (Move arms back and forth)

The children on the bus go bumpity-bump,
Bumpity-bump, bumpity-bump.
The children on the bus go bumpity-bump,
All through the town. (Children move up and down)

The babies on the bus go "Waa, waa, waa,
Waa, waa, waa, waa, waa, waa."
The babies on the bus go "Waa, waa, waa,"
All through the town. (Pretend to rub eyes)

The mothers on the bus go 'Shh, shh, shh,
Shh, shh, shh, shh, shh, shh."
The mothers on the bus go "Shh, shh, shh,"
All through the town. (Hold finger to lips)

The fathers on the busy say, "Look at that,
Look at that, look at that."
The fathers on the bus say, "Look at that,"
All through the town. (Point at objects)

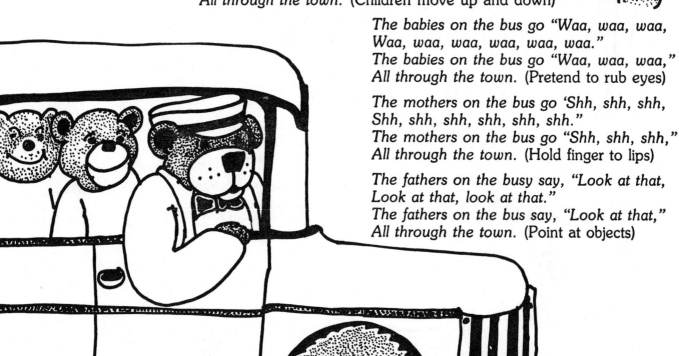

NARRATOR: "Listen carefully to the alphabet song. The children are going to want you to do something with them when they are finished."

ABC SONG

A B C D E F G H I J K L M N O P Q R S T U V W X Y and Z
I can say my a b c's.
Next time won't you sing with me.
(Repeat the alphabet song with the audience.)

NARRATOR: "The rhythm of music helps us move. (The children form a circle.) They will walk, run, skip, etc. to the beat of a drum. They will start by walking as I beat the drum slowly. (Do it.) Now I'm going to beat it a little faster. Watch the children move more quickly to keep pace with the beat. Now watch them as I change the beat once more." (Slow the beat to a quiet pace and have the children tip-toe to their mats.)

NARRATOR: "I bet you didn't know that you carry a band with you all of the time. Listen as the children play their 'Body Band.'

THE BODY BAND

Beat, beat with your feet,
We're playing the body band.

Strum, strum with your thumb,
It's the best one in the land.

Clap, clap on your lap,
Keep rhythm with your knees.

Hear, hear with your ear,
Stop laughing if you please.

Cluck, cluck like a duck,
It's fun on a rainy day.

Pop, pop on your top,
Keep humming as you play.

Moan, moan all alone,
You're playing your solo now.

Haste, haste with your waist,
It's time to take your bow!

by Dick Wilmes

NARRATOR: "Mood music relaxes us and helps us rest. This is an all time favorite."

ROCK-A-BYE-BABY

Rock-a-bye-baby in the tree top.
When the wind blows, the cradle will rock.
When the bough breaks, the cradle will fall.
Down will come baby, cradle and all.

NARRATOR: "Today we have a special guest who will share his/her musical talent with us." (Introduce the special guest/s.)

NARRATOR: "Thank you for joining in our musical fun. The children have made two snacks named after familiar tunes, Muffin Man Muffins and Shoo Fly Butter. Please come and enjoy them with a Glass of Milk."

THE MAGIC OF MOTHER GOOSE

Teacher . . . . Welcome
Children Enter . . . . Walking to the Beat of Nursery Rhyme Music
London Bridge . . . . All Children
Little Miss Muffet . . . . Two Children
Little Boy Blue . . . . Child
Jack and Jill . . . . Two Children
Humpty Dumpty . . . . Several Children
Little Jack Horner . . . . Child
Three Little Kittens . . . . . . All Children
Little Bo Peep . . . . Child
Mary, Mary Quite Contrary . Child
Hickory, Dickory Dock . . . . Child
Jack Be Nimble . . . . Child
See Saw Majorie Daw . . . . . Child
Mary Had A Little Lamb . . . Two Children
Ring Around the Rosie . . . . All Children
Refreshments

Program Covers — Fold pieces of dark blue construction paper in half and stencil a goose on the front cover of each one. To make the stencils cut several goose shapes out of lightweight posterboard. Have the children lay a stencil on the cover of each program. Using a brush-type shoe polish applicator bottle, have the children brush white polish around the edges of the stencil. When they have finished, they should carefully lift the stencil and let the polish dry.

PREPARATION

Children's Planning:

• Enjoy a unit concentrating on nursery rhymes.

• After the unit let the children choose their favorite nursery rhymes.

Classroom Preparation:

• Enjoy reciting the rhymes during the unit.

• Give each child several opportunities to pantomime his favorite rhymes.

Songs and Fingerplays: The list of nursery rhymes may be shortened or lengthened depending on the number of children in your class. You can also have several children pantomiming each one.

- *London Bridge*
- *Little Miss Muffet*
- *Little Boy Blue*
- *Jack and Jill*
- *Humpty Dumpty*
- *Little Jack Horner*
- *Three Little Kittens*
- *Little Bo Peep*
- *Mary, Mary Quite Contrary*
- *Hickory, Dickory Dock*
- *Jack Be Nimble*
- *See Saw Marjorie Daw*
- *Mary Had a Little Lamb*
- *Ring Around the Rosie*

Costumes: Costumes are optional. If they are worn send a note home to the parents several weeks before the program telling them what character their child has chosen to be and a costume suggestion.

Rhyme	Costumes	Props
Mother Goose	Long skirt, large hat tied down	
Little Miss Muffet	Spider has 4 paper legs taped to child's legs	Bowl, spoon, stool
Little Boy Blue	Hat	Horn, haystack (made from blocks)
Jack and Jill		Pail
Humpty Dumpty		Classroom blocks
Little Jack Horner		Stool, pie pan, playdough plum
Three Little Kittens	Real mittens for each child	Clothesline, clothespins
Little Bo Peep		Teaching staff are the sheep and they wear paper bag masks
Mary, Mary Quite Contrary		Watering can, flowers
Hickory, Dickory Dock	Mouse has gray paper ears and a rope tail	Clock held by child
Jack Be Nimble		Candle and holder
See Saw Majorie Daw		Teeter totter
Mary Had a Little Lamb		Stuffed lamb

Nametags: Geese

Decorations: Get a large refrigerator box. Cut it diagonally across the top and bottom. Cut down opposite sides so that the box is cut in half and forms two corners. Use one corner to make an open book. On the outside cover write 'The Magic of Mother Goose.' On the inside left-hand page write 'Stars' and list all of the children's names. Cut the center of the back page out leaving an 8″ rim all the way around.

Set-up:

- The children's mats are arranged on the two sides of the presentation area.

- The large book is placed in the middle, leaving room in front for the children to pantomime, dance, and sing.

- You'll need a recording of London Bridge.

- Put all of the props in place.

- Arrange with an adult to set-up and remove the props for each rhyme.

- Arrange with two adults to form the arch during the children's entrance.

- Have mittens on the children's mats.

- Hang a clothesline off to one side of the presentation area for the children to use during 'Three Little Kittens.' Have clothespins clipped to the line.

Refreshments: Little Jack Horner Pies and Juice.

Little Jack Horner Pies

You'll Need:
2 loaves frozen whole
    wheat bread

Glaze — optional
½ cup powdered sugar
1 Tbs milk

To Make: Thaw and follow the directions for rising. Have the children form the bread into golf ball size balls. Continue to follow the directions for rising and baking. After the Little Jack Horner Pies have cooled, they may be glazed.

PRESENTATION

MOTHER GOOSE: Welcome to Storyland. From the pages of my famous book I bring you magic. Just take a look at each new page and see the characters come alive before your very eyes!

Children enter in pairs walking briskly to the music of 'London Bridge.' Two adults form an arch in the presentation area. The children walk under the arch and go to their mats. They can sing along with the recording until all of the children have gone under the arch.

MOTHER GOOSE: "On page 1 is Little Miss Muffet seated on her favorite tuffet." (An adult puts the stool in place. Miss Muffet comes forward and walks behind the book, enters through the page and sits on the stool. The children recite the verse as she pantomimes. The spider runs up to Little Miss Muffet at the appropriate time and sits down beside her. Remove props.)

LITTLE MISS MUFFET

Little Miss Muffet sat on a tuffet,
Eating her curds and whey,
There came a great spider and sat down beside her,
And frightened Miss Muffet away!

MOTHER GOOSE: "On page 2 is Little Boy Blue. Whatever is he going to do?" (Add props in front of the book. Little Boy Blue walks behind the book, steps through, and leans against a haystack as the children recite his verse. Remove props.)

LITTLE BOY BLUE

Little Boy Blue come blow your horn,
The sheep's in the meadow,
The cow's in the corn.
Where is the little boy who looks after the sheep?
Under the haystack, fast asleep.

MOTHER GOOSE: "On page 3 Jack and Jill are having a hard time on the hill." (Jack and Jill walk to the back of the book. They pick up a pail and step through the page. As the group recites the poem, they pantomime. Leave the pail behind the book.)

JACK AND JILL

Jack and Jill went up the hill
To fetch a pail of water.
Jack fell down and broke his crown
And Jill came tumbling after.

MOTHER GOOSE: "On page 4 we see Humpty Dumpty building a wall. Be careful Humpty so it doesn't fall." (Add props. Humpty Dumpty builds a wall in front of the book using 6-9 large cardboard blocks. He sits on the wall and pantomimes as the group recites the poem. Remove props.)

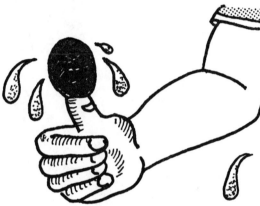

HUMPTY DUMPTY

Humpty Dumpty sat on a wall.
Humpty Dumpty had a great fall.
All the king's horses and all the king's men,
Couldn't put Humpty together again.

MOTHER GOOSE: "Look what is on page 5. Little Jack Horner and his Christmas pie." (Add props. Jack Horner sits on a stool in front of the book with his pie in his lap and a playdough plum on his thumb. Remove props.)

LITTLE JACK HORNER

Little Jack Horner sat in a corner,
Eating his Christmas pie;
He put in his thumb
And pulled out a plum.
And said, "Oh, what a good boy am I!"

MOTHER GOOSE: "I think that I'm on page number 6 with a Mother Cat and her many kittens." (All of the children stand. Mother Goose slowly recites the poem dramatizing the Mother Cat part. The children are the kittens. They pantomime as Mother Goose reads their parts. First they loose their mittens by hiding them under the mat. Then they find them and put them on. Mother pretends to give them pie and they pretend to eat it. They soil their mittens and she scolds them. They pretend to wash and then hang the mittens on the line to dry. The mother is pleased.)

_____ LITTLE KITTENS
(Use the number of children in your class.)

Narrator: Three little kittens, they lost their mittens,
And they began to cry,
Kittens: "Oh, mother dear, we sadly fear
That we have lost our mittens."

Mother: "What! Lost your mittens, you naughty kittens!
Then you shall have no pie.
Mee-ow, mee-ow, mee-ow.
No, you shall have no pie."

Narrator: The three little kittens, they found their mittens,
And they began to cry,
Kittens: "Oh, mother dear, see here, see here,
For we have found our mittens."

Mother: "What! Found your mittens, you silly kittens!
Then you shall have some pie.
Purr-r, purr-r, purr-r,
Oh, let us have some pie."

Narrator: The three little kittens put on their mittens,
And soon ate up the pie.
Kittens: "Oh, mother dear, we greatly fear
That we have soiled our mittens."

Mother: "What! Soiled your mittens, you naughty kittens!"
Then they began to sigh,
"Mee-ow, mee-ow, mee-ow."
Then they began to sigh.

Narrator: The three little kittens they washed their mittens,
And hung them out to dry.
Kittens: "Oh, mother dear, do you not hear,
That we have washed our mittens?"

Mother: "What! Washed your mittens? You're good kittens.
But I smell a rat close by.
Mee-ow, mee-ow, mee-ow.
I smell a rat close by."

MOTHER GOOSE: "On page number 7 we happen to meet Little Bo Peep and two lost sheep. (Little Bo Peep walks through the book as though looking for her lost sheep. The sheep (the teaching staff) appear as the children say "Leave them alone . . . them.")

LITTLE BO PEEP

Little Bo Peep has lost her sheep
And doesn't know where to find them.
Leave them alone and they'll come home,
Wagging their tails behind them.

MOTHER GOOSE: "Mary, Mary Quite Contrary is on page 8. Let's hurry now, she doesn't like to be late." (Mary walks behind the book, comes out of the page with the empty watering can and pretends to water flowers as the verse is being recited.)

MARY, MARY QUITE CONTRARY

Mary, Mary quite contrary
How does your garden grow?
With silver bells and cockle shells
And pretty maids all in a row.

MOTHER GOOSE: "I think I hear tick, tick, tock. Could it be Hickory, Dickory Dock?" (The mouse, Hickory, and the child who strikes 'one' walk behind the book where Hickory and the child are given their props. When the poem begins they walk through the book. Hickory holds the clock and the mouse runs around it. When the clock 'strikes one' the child with the wood blocks claps them together.)

HICKORY, DICKORY DOCK

Hickory, Dickory Dock!
The mouse ran up the clock.
The clock struck one.
The mouse ran down.
Hickory, Dickory Dock!

MOTHER GOOSE: "On page 10 a candle I spy, Jack must be very spry." (The candlestick is placed in front of the book. Jack jumps back and forth as the poem is said. Remove props.)

JACK BE NIMBLE

Jack be nimble, Jack be quick
Jack jump over the candlestick.

MOTHER GOOSE: "On page 11 there is a see-saw as it was called in Marjorie Daw." (Add props. Two children each sit on an end of a board with a balance in the middle. Remove props.)

SEE SAW MARJORIE DAW

See-saw, Marjorie Daw
Johnnie shall have a new master,
He shall have but a penny a day
Because he can't work any faster.

MOTHER GOOSE: "On page 12 there is a surprise. Mary and her lamb are before our eyes. (Mary walks behind the book and comes out with a real or stuffed lamb as children sing the verse.)

MARY HAD A LITTLE LAMB

Mary had a little lamb, little lamb, little lamb
Mary had a little lamb, its fleece was white as snow.
Everywhere that Mary went, Mary went, Mary went
Everywhere that Mary went, the lamb was sure to go.

MOTHER GOOSE: "Before I close my book today, I have a game that we really must play. All of the children should join hands.

RING AROUND THE ROSIE

Ring around the rosie
Pockets full of posies,
Ashes, ashes we all fall down.

MOTHER GOOSE: "Thank you for coming and sharing our fun. Now we'd like you to try our Little Jack Horner Pies and a Glass of Milk."

ONE, TWO BUCKLE MY SHOE

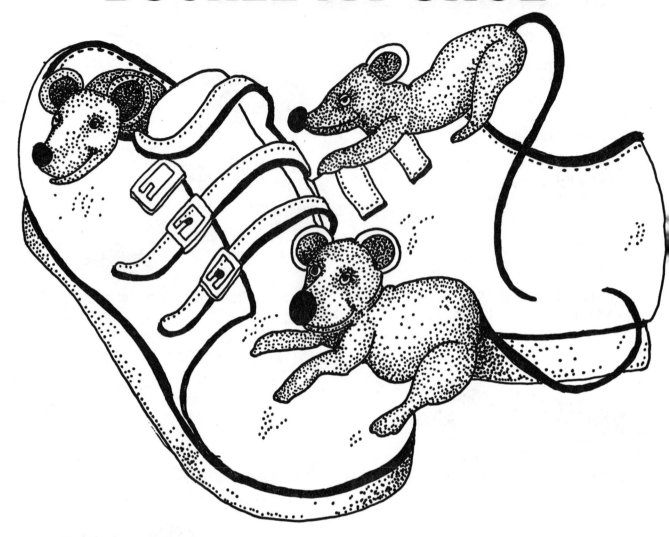

Children Enter . . . . Children Walk in With Their Numbered Balloons
Teacher . . . . Welcome
Activity . . . . Balloon Sale
Rhyme . . . . *One, Two Buckle My Shoe*
Rhyme . . . . *There Were Five In a Bed*
Story . . . . Three Billy Goats Gruff
Dance . . . . Triangle, Circle, and Square
Fingerplay . . . . *One Is For the Rocket*
Refreshments

Program Covers — Using construction paper, have the children cut
three balloon shapes for each program. Glue them on the cover and
number them 1, 2, and 3.

PREPARATION

Children's Planning:

- The children can help decide what songs and fingerplays they would like to perform, along with the number games they would like to teach their families.

- Read the story of the 'Three Billy Goats Gruff.'

Classroom Preparation:

- Review the games, songs, and activities as needed.

- Review the 'Three Billy Goats Gruff' if you are going to dramatize it or let the children know what felt character each will put on the board.

- Have each child cut a large circle, square, or triangle from a 9"x12" piece of brightly colored construction paper. They will use these with the song, 'Triangle, Circle, and Square.'

- Practice the dance for 'Triangle, Circle, and Square.' Each child holds a shape during the song. During the first verse, children holding circles come forward, form a small circle, and move around in a circle until the chorus begins. During the chorus, each child holds up his shape as it is named in the song. During the second verse, children holding squares form a square and march around. Repeat the chorus. During the third verse, children holding triangles form a triangle and march. Repeat the chorus.

- Have the children cut balloon shapes from different colors of construction paper and attach them to paint stir-sticks. Using a wide marker the teacher should write a numeral on each one. (If you have access to helium, you might want to use helium balloons instead of paper ones.)

Songs and Fingerplays:

- *One, Two Buckle My Shoe*
- *There Were Five In a Bed*
- *One Is For the Rocket*

Costumes: None

Nametags: Balloons

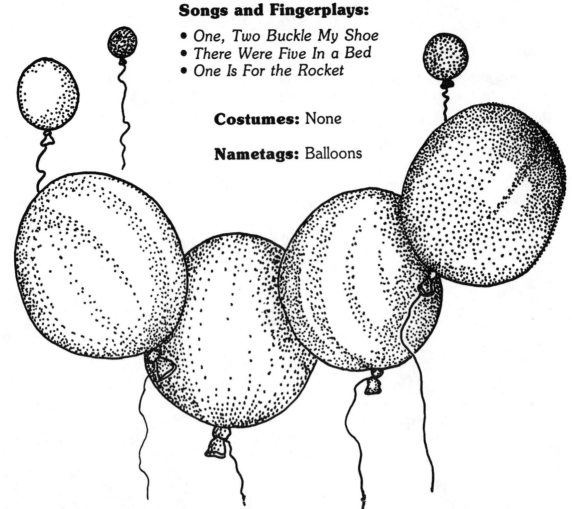

Decorations: Use number and shape posters along with the children's artwork.

Set-up:

- Spread the children's mats in the presentation area. Put their shapes on their mats.

- Get a recording of 'Triangle, Circle, and Square' from the Hap Palmer album, *Learning Basic Skills Through Music, Volume II*.

- Get a copy of the story 'The Three Billy Goats Gruff.' Make the felt characters for the story. Have your felt board nearby.

Refreshments: 1, 2, 3 Punch and Number Pretzels. The children can prepare the Number Pretzels the day before the program.

1, 2, 3 Punch

You'll Need:

1 pkg unsweetened cherry Kool-Aid (Mix according to directions)

2 qts gingerale

3 different kinds of frozen juices (1 6oz can of frozen lemonade, orange and pineapple. Mix according to the directions.)

To Make: During the morning of the program, mix all of the above ingredients except the gingerale. Just before serving add the gingerale. Serves about 50.

Number Pretzels

You'll Need:
1 pkg yeast
1 tsp sugar
1½ cups warm water
1 tsp salt
4 cups sifted flour
1 beaten egg
Coarse salt

To Make: Add the sugar and salt to the warm water. Sprinkle the yeast on the water and let dissolve. Blend in the flour. Knead the dough on a floured surface until smooth. Roll out the dough. Cut it into strips. Roll the strips and form them into numerals. Place on a greased cookie sheet. Brush with egg. Sprinkle with salt if desired. Bake at 425° for 15 minutes. Makes 30-40 small pretzels.

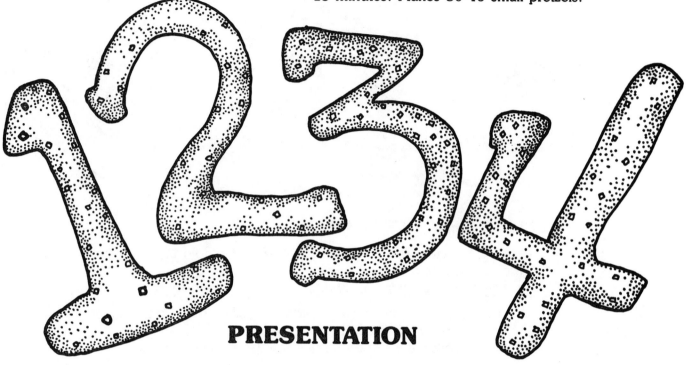

PRESENTATION

Children march in chanting, "Hup, two, three, four; hup, two, three, four," with their numbered balloons in the air.

Teacher welcomes the group.

NARRATOR: "Numbers are an important part of all aspects of our lives today. Even marching in was easier because we used numbers. In school we learn numbers and math concepts in every area of our curriculum. Today we will show you how we incorporate numbers into our day. Our first activity 'The Balloon Sale' gives the children practice in recognizing numerals. Watch as I buy a bunch of balloons. I would like to buy a balloon with the numeral '2.' Now I need one with a numeral '7'." (Each child hands the adult a balloon as she says his numeral. When all of the balloons have been collected they are bunched together to make a balloon bouquet and placed in a square of styrofoam. Reassure the children that they will get their balloons back at the end of the program.)

NARRATOR: "We also learn about numbers through poems and songs. Listen to the children enjoying, 'One, Two Buckle My Shoe' and 'Five in a Bed'."

93

ONE, TWO BUCKLE MY SHOE

One, two buckle my shoe
Three, four knock at the door
Five, six pick up sticks
Seven, eight lay them straight
Nine, ten a good fat hen.

THERE WERE FIVE IN A BED

There were 5 in a bed and the little one said, (Hold up 5 fingers)
"Roll over, roll over" (Roll arms)
So they all rolled over and one fell out. (Put down thumb)

There were 4 in the bed and the little one said, (Hold up 4 fingers)
"Roll over, roll over" (Roll arms)
So they all rolled over and one fell out. (Put down pointer)

Continue: There were 3 in the bed
           There were 2 in the bed
           There was 1 in the bed and the little one said,
           "Good night!"
         by Tonja Evetts-Weimer

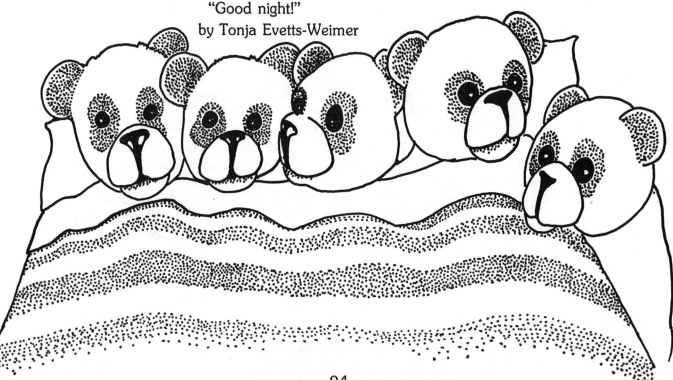

NARRATOR: "The story of the 'Three Billy Goats Gruff' helps the children to understand size." (As the narrator reads the story have the children add characters to the felt board at appropriate times and make the noises of the goats, trip-tropping across the bridge. If you decide to dramatize it, have the children act out the parts.)

NARRATOR: "Shape is another aspect of math. The children have practiced a dance to accompany the song called, 'Triangle, Circle, and Square'." (Each child should pick up his shape and then begin the dance when the recording starts.)

NARRATOR: "With computers and our advanced space programs we know that numbers will always be important in our lives."

ONE IS FOR THE ROCKET

One is for the rocket standing straight and tall.
Two is for the stages, count them as they fall.
Three is for the cameras watching earth below.
Four is for the weightlessness which makes us float so slow.
Five is for the astronauts ready for the trip.
Six is for the space food packaged not to tip.
Seven is for the telescopes to study a far off star.
Eight is for the satellites to be launched from afar.
Nine is for the instruments to help the research team.
Ten is for the countdown ready to begin.
10, 9, 8, 7, 6, 5, 4, 3, 2, 1, BLAST-OFF!!!
       by Susan Spaete

NARRATOR: "We learn about numbers in our baking activities, too. Today we have made 1, 2, 3 Punch and Number Pretzels for you. Please join us.

LET'S WORK OUT

Children Enter	Walk to the Obstacle Course
Teacher	Welcome
Activity	Obstacle Course
Game	Circle Kick
Activity	Parachute
Game	Relay (With Older Children)
Dance	Movement Record
Game	Flag Game (With Older Children)
Refreshments	

Program Covers — Have the children cut 5″ construction paper circles. Using a marble painting technique, paint each circle a variety of colors to look like a ball. When dry, glue the balls to the covers.

PREPARATION

Children's Planning:

• After learning many active games, let the children help choose their favorite ones to play during the program.

Classroom Preparation:

• For several weeks before the program, practice the activities during regular large muscle periods.

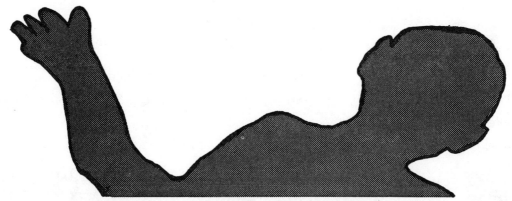

• Have the children decorate full body tracings of themselves. To do this the children lie down on pieces of butcher paper and pretend to be doing a movement, such as clapping their hands over their heads. Trace around the child and let him decorate his shape with markers. While he is coloring, ask him what movement he is doing. Write it on an index card and staple it to a hand on the tracing. Tape the children's tracings to your wall.

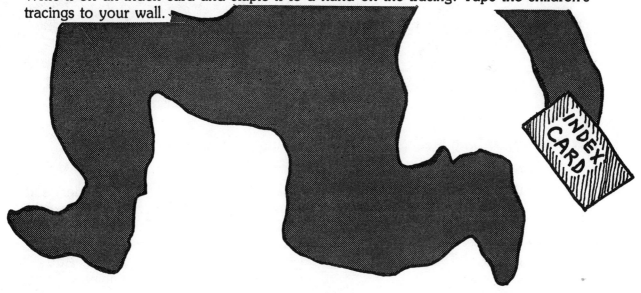

Songs and Fingerplays: None

Costumes: Exercise suits, jogging suits, shorts and gym shoes.

Nametags: Barbells

Decorations: Classroom artwork including the body tracings described above.

Set-up:

- This program requires a lot of space and should take place in a gym or large room. If you do not have such a room, contact your local 'Y,' elementary school, or other such facility.

- The obstacle course should be set-up ahead of time.

- Ask parents to help you with the six stations along the obstacle course.

- All of the equipment (beanbags, automobile tires, dowel rods, ladder, bicycle tires or hula hoops, tumbling mat, balance beam) and a brief set of directions should be within easy reach of the people leading the games and activities at the different stations.

- Select any song you like to play during the 'Circle Kick' game.

- Have a rubber playground ball for the 'Circle Kick' game.

- You'll need a parachute, drum, and beanbags for parachute activities.

- You'll need a recording of 'Listen and Move' by Greg Scelesa and Steve Millang, *We All Live Together, Volume II.*

- If you play the two games for the older children, you'll need beanbags and flags.

Refreshments: Bran Muffins and Carrot-Pineapple Juice.

Bran Muffins

You'll Need:
2½ cups flour
2 Tbs baking powder
½ tsp salt
¼ cup + 2 Tbs honey
½ cup sugar
3 cups bran cereal
2½ cups milk
2 eggs
½ cup vegetable oil

To Make: Stir the flour, baking powder, and salt together. Set aside. Measure the cereal and milk in a large bowl. Stir together and let stand for one or two minutes until softened. Add honey, eggs and oil. Beat well. Add flour mixture, stir only until combined. Pour the batter into muffin cups. Bake at 375° for 18-20 minutes or until done. Yields 24-28 regular size muffins or 48 smaller ones.

Carrot/Pineapple Juice

You'll Need:
Carrots
Unsweetened pineapple juice
Cracked ice

To Make: Wash the carrots. Cut them up into small pieces. In a blender mix the carrots and the pineapple juice. Add the cracked ice and blend at high speed. Add a carrot stick to each drink for a stirrer.

98

PRESENTATION

Children walk in and go to one of the stations along the obstacle course.

Teacher welcomes everyone to 'Let's Work Out.'

NARRATOR: "The first activity is our obstacle course. There are six stations along the course. The children will progress through all of them. There is an adult at each station to assist the children."

STATION 1

Beanbag Toss — Have the children toss the beanbags underhand into some automobile tires that are positioned close together and others that are spread farther apart.

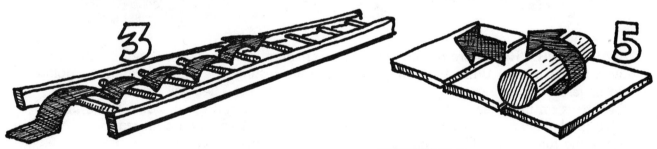

STATION 6

Balance Beam — Have the children walk forward to the end of the beam and then walk backwards to the starting point.

STATION 2

Low Bars — The children should crawl under the bars (dowel rods) on their stomachs the first time and jump over them on the way back.

STATION 5

The Mat — Have the children lie down and do log rolls with their arms at their sides.

STATION 3

Ladder on the Floor — Starting at one end, the children should jump, with their feet together over each of the rungs, turn around and walk back through the rungs to the starting point.

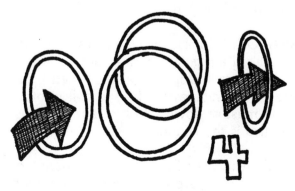

STATION 4

Bicycle Tires — Jump through the bicycle tires (hula hoops) which have been set-up in a maze.

NARRATOR: "Now that the children have stretched all of their muscles, they are ready to play 'Circle Kick.' This game strengthens their leg muscles. (The children form a circle. They sit down, placing their hands towards the outside of the circle.) Using only their feet, they will try to keep the ball from going out of the circle by kicking it when it comes their way. The game begins when I start the record. Each time I stop the record, the children should stop kicking. The game ends when the record is over."

NARRATOR: "The parachute strengthens the children's hand and shoulder muscles. (Adults and children position themselves around the parachute.) You are going to enjoy several activities together. First you are going to walk around in a circle to the beat of the drum." (Beat at different rhythms.)

- Holding the chute with one hand, thumbs up, walk around in a circle. Chant, "Walk, walk, walk," at different speeds as you move. Stop.

- Facing the middle and using two hands, lift the parachute in place. Stop.

- Shake the rug. Faster. Slower, slower, slower. Stop.

- Make popcorn by shaking beanbags out of the popper (the parachute). Stop.

- Make large waves. Stop.

- Make a dome shape (mushroom). Stop.

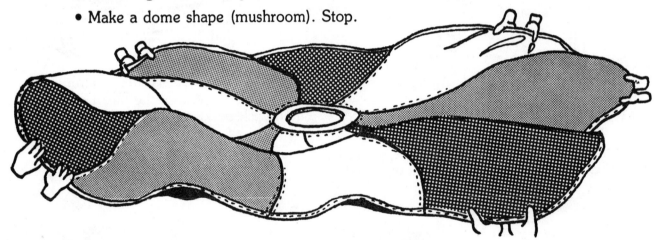

NARRATOR: "Relays are popular with older children. (Have the younger children sit with their parents.) While the younger children are resting, the older children are going to have a beanbag race. (Older children form two teams.) They will balance the beanbags on their heads, move quickly to the marker, turn around, come back, and give the beanbag to a team member. The race is completed when both teams have gone the full circuit." (To extend or change this, the children can balance the beanbags on their right or left forearms or on their shoulders.)

NARRATOR: "Everyone form a large circle or several smaller ones. Listen carefully as the record, 'Listen and Move' tells you different ways to move around the circle. We'll begin with walking." (Begin the recording.)

NARRATOR: "Our last activity is also for the older children. It involves using several motor skills. I am going to give each child a flag to put in his pocket. (Do it.) I'll give the order to walk, skip, or gallop. When I do, the children should begin moving (define the boundaries) and try to collect other children's flags. If a flag is taken from a child, he must sit down. No hands may be used to protect the flags. The child with the last flag is the winner."

NARRATOR: "We all know the importance of exercise. I hope that you've all enjoyed exercising at today's program. Please join us for Bran Muffins and a Glass of Carrot-Pineapple Juice."

BUGS, SPIDERS, AND CRAWLY THINGS

Teacher	Welcome
Children Enter	Children Flutter in to the Music From 'Flight of the Bumble Bee' by Rimsky-Korsakov
Bee	*What Do You Suppose* *Here Is the Beehive*
Spiders	*Eensy Weensy Spider*
Grasshopper	*Grasshopper Green*
Caterpillar	Drama: 'A Very Hungry Caterpillar'
Ants	*The Ants Go Marching*
Ladybug	*Meet Ladybug*
Fly	*Skip To My Lou*
Refreshments	

Program Covers — Using an ink pad or a shallow pan of paint, have the children press one of their fingers onto the pad and then press it onto construction paper. Make several prints. When dry, the children can add features to their prints such as legs, antennae, etc. Create several insects on each program. When complete, fold the paper in half and insert the program information inside.

PREPARATION

Children's Planning:

• Enjoy a unit about bugs, spiders, and other crawly things.

• After the unit have each child choose one of his favorite crawly things.

Classroom Preparation:

• Review the rhymes and songs the children learned during the unit.

• Read the story of *The Very Hungry Caterpillar,* by Eric Carle.

• Have the children create large pictures of their favorite insects. Pre-cut or let the children cut large circles and ovals to use as bodies for the insects. They can use collage materials for antennae, markings, legs, eyes, etc.

• The children can prepare large construction paper objects similar to those in the book, *The Very Hungry Caterpillar.*

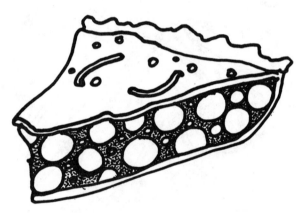

— 1 24″x12″ leaf with a white cotton ball glued on
— 1 12″x12″ caterpillar
— 1 24″x12″ red apple
— 2 24″x12″ green or yellow pears
— 3 24″x12″ blue or purple plums
— 4 24″x12″ red strawberries
— 5 24″x12″ orange oranges
— 1 24″x12″ brown chocolate cake
— 1 24″x12″ ice cream cone
— 1 24″x12″ green pickle
— 1 24″x12″ yellow swiss cheese
— 1 24″x12″ pink salami slice
— 1 24″x12″ lollipop
— 1 24″x12″ cherry pie
— 1 24″x12″ sausage
— 1 24″x12″ cupcake
— 1 24″x12″ watermelon slice
— 1 24″x12″ green leaf with 2-3, 3½ holes
— 1 24″x6″ large caterpillar
— 1 24″x12″ brown cocoon (large enough to cover the large caterpillar)
— 1 butterfly made from two 12″x24″ pieces of brightly colored paper

- Have the children form spiders by bending four black pipe cleaners and overlapping them to form eight legs. Attach a long piece of heavy, black thread to the middle of each spider. Hang them from your ceiling.

Songs and Fingerplays:

- *What Do You Suppose*
- *Here Is the Beehive*
- *Eensy Weensy Spider*
- *Grasshopper Green*
- *The Ants Go Marching*
- *Meet Ladybug*
- *Skip To My Lou*

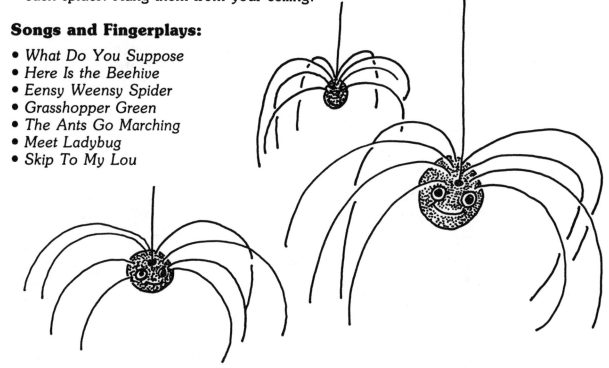

Costumes: Have all of the children make bumblebee headbands. Cut 2" wide strips of corrugated cardboard to fit each child's head. Let each child paint his headband. When it is dry, poke several pipe cleaners into the corrugation. The children can bend the pipe cleaners any direction they would like. Tape or staple the headbands together.

Nametags: Butterflies

Decorations:

- Use the children's art that they created during the unit. In addition have several insect collections on display.

- Hang three-dimensional objects, including the children's pipe cleaner spiders from the ceiling. You might also want to hang 'Clothespin Butterflies' and 'Egg Carton Caterpillars.' To make a butterfly paint a spring-loaded clothespin. While it is drying, cut three 4"x5" squares of tissue paper. Gather the paper in the middle and slide into the clothespin. Add pipe cleaner antennae. Attach a string and hang. To make the caterpillar, paint egg carton sections and add antennae with toothpicks. Attach strings and hang from the ceiling.

Set-up:

- Print the children's names on strips of masking tape. Fasten the strips to the floor where the children will have their mats to stand and sit on.

- On their mats put the large insect pictures which the children created.

- Have the book, *The Very Hungry Caterpillar* by Eric Carle available. Place the props for the story on the children's mats.

- You'll need a recording of the *'Flight of the Bumblebee.'*

Refreshments: Ants on a Log, Butterfly Sandwiches, and Bug Juice.

Ants on a Log

You'll Need:
Celery
Peanut butter
Raisins

To Make: Wash the celery. Cut the stalks into short pieces. Stuff the pieces with peanut butter. Dot each piece with raisins.

Bug Juice

You'll Need:
1 6oz can lemonade
1 6oz can limeade
1 6oz can pineapple
1 pkg unsweetened lime
  Kool-Aid
2 qts gingerale (optional)

To Make: Mix all of the juices and Kool-Aid with water as directed on the container. Blend them. If you're going to add the gingerale, do it just before serving. Makes about 50, 4 oz. servings.

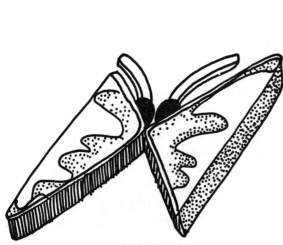
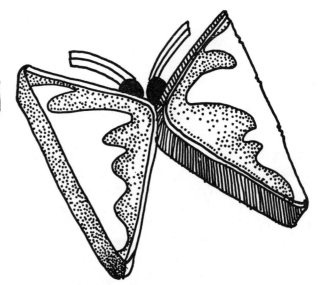

Butterfly Sandwiches

You'll Need:
Bread
Cream cheese
Food coloring
Olives
Raisins
Celery bits
Carrot sticks

To Make: Spread cream cheese that has been colored with slight amounts of food coloring on the bread. Cut the bread diagonally in half. Pair the breads to form butterfly wings. Decorate with food pieces and add carrot stick antennae to each one.

PRESENTATION

Children wearing their bumblebee headbands flutter in as 'The Flight of the Bumblebee' is playing in the background. While they flutter in, they can also make soft buzzing sounds.

TEACHER: "Welcome to our program about bugs, spiders, and crawly things. We have learned about the delicate balance of nature and the place for insects and spiders in our world. The children have each chosen their favorite insect or spider and have drawn pictures of them. They will display these as they sing, dance and tell stories about them."

NARRATOR: "We learned that bees are important for pollinating plants and making honey. We will say two bee rhymes for you. The children who liked bees the best will hold up their pictures." (As the children are saying, 'What Do You Suppose' have those children who created bumblebees hold their pictures up.)

WHAT DO YOU SUPPOSE

What do you suppose?
A bee sat on my nose.
(Touch thumb and first two fingers together, flutter hand, and land on nose.)
Then what do you think?
He gave me a wink. (Wink one eye)
And said, "I beg your pardon,
I thought you were the garden."
(Make flying-away motions with hands.)
         from Kidstuff

HERE IS THE BEEHIVE

Here is the beehive. (Make a fist)
Where are the bees? (Look at fist)
Hiding inside where nobody sees?
Look! They are coming
Out of their hive. (Loosen fingers gradually)
One, two, three, four, five. (Hold up each finger in succession)

NARRATOR: "Spiders are not insects, but they are helpful. We will now say the rhyme 'The Eensy Weensy Spider' as those who liked spiders best show their pictures. (Have the children hold up their pictures.) Those of you who know the rhyme please join us."

EENSY WEENSY SPIDER

The eensy weensy spider (Opposite thumb and pointer fingers touching)
Climbed up the waterspout. (Climb fingers upward)
Down came the rain (Flutter fingers downward)
And washed the spider out. (Sweep hands outward)
Out came the sun (Form a circle overhead)
And dried up all the rain (Palms held up)
And the eensy weensy spider (Repeat first movement)
Climbed up the spout again.

NARRATOR: "The grasshopper seems like a cheerful, carefree insect. The children who drew grasshoppers will now show them to you as we do our grasshopper activity.

GRASSHOPPER GREEN

The grasshopper's such a comical chap,
He lives on the best of fare.
Bright green trousers, jacket, and cap,
These are his summerwear.

Skipperty, skopperty, high and low
Summer's the time for fun.
(While saying the chorus, the children should put their hands on their hips and jump in place.)

Under the hedge he loves to go
As soon as the day's begun.
Out in the grass with a heigh, heigh, ho,
Playing away in the sun.

Skipperty, skopperty, high and low
Summer's the time for fun.

The grasshopper sings a merry song,
He's calling the children to play
He frisks and frolics all day long
He's oh, so happy and gay.

Skipperty, skopperty, high and low
Summer's the time for fun.
        from Kidstuff

106

NARRATOR: "The children will now act out a story we have read in class, *The Very Hungry Caterpillar* by Eric Carle." (Have the children pick up the props from their mats and stand in line according to the sequence of the story. As the story is being read the children show how the little caterpillar changed into a beautiful butterfly. The child with the small caterpillar puts it through the holes of the food as the narrator reads the story. The child holding each food picture takes the small caterpillar from behind his picture and gives it to the child who continues to insert it through all of the foods and the large leaf. The child holding the leaf should conceal a large caterpillar behind it. When the small caterpillar enters the hole, the large caterpillar is given to the child and the small one remains hidden behind the leaf. The butterfly is folded behind the cocoon. The large caterpillar is put behind the cocoon. When the last page is read, the child who has been holding the caterpillar takes the butterfly out and flutters it away.)

NARRATOR: "The ant is a very hard worker. Our story is called, 'The Ants Go Marching.' Those that liked ants the best will now show you their pictures."

THE ANTS GO MARCHING

The ants go marching one by one hurrah, hurrah
The ants go marching one by one hurrah, hurrah
The ants go marching one by one, the little one stops to suck his thumb
(Suck thumbs)
And they all go marching down, around the town.
Boom, boom, boom (March one finger)

Continue using 2, 3, 4, and 5 fingers.

NARRATOR: "A favorite of many children is the ladybug. It almost seems tame when it lands on your hand in the summer."

MEET LADYBUG

Meet ladybug . . . (Thumb)
Here is little sister Sadie Bug (Pointer)
Her mother is Mrs. Grady Bug (Middle finger)
Her aunt, that nice old ladybug (Ring finger)
And baby . . . she's a little fraidy bug. (Baby finger)

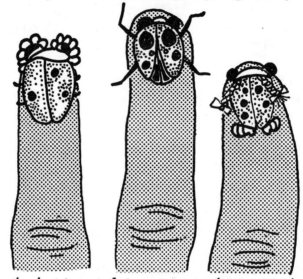

NARRATOR: "The fly is the last insect. It is not a popular insect. Actually we would like to get rid of it when we see it. In our last act the children will sing and dance to shoo those flies away."

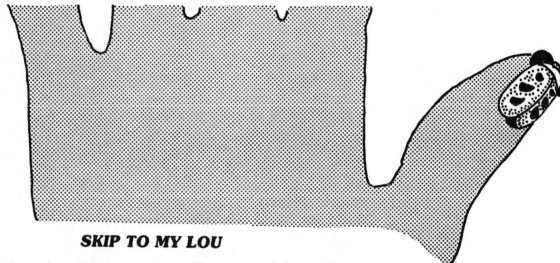

SKIP TO MY LOU

Skip, skip, skip to my Lou, (Skip around the circle)
Skip, skip, skip to my Lou,
Skip,. skip, skip to my Lou,
Skip to my Lou my darlin'.

Flies in the buttermilk, shoo fly, shoo,
(Stand facing partner, stomp feet, and shoo flies by opening and closing their fingers)
Flies in the buttermilk, shoo fly, shoo.
Flies in the buttermilk, shoo fly, shoo.
Skip to my Lou my darlin'. (Hold hands and skip out)

NARRATOR: "I hope you have a better understanding of bugs, spiders, and other crawly things from today's program. We will be serving refreshments. Don't be afraid to try some Butterfly Sandwiches, Ants on a Log, and Bug Juice. Thank you."

DINOSAUR DOINGS

Children Enter . . . . Lumber in to the Beginning of
Prokofiev's 'Peter and the Wolf'
Teacher . . . . Welcome
Song . . . . *All About Dinosaurs*
Demonstration . . . . Children Tell About Their Dinosaur Models
Song . . . . *I'm Bringing Home a Baby Dinosaur*
Rhyme . . . . *The Ill-Mannered Dinosaur*
Activities . . . . Dinosaur Games, Puzzles, Stories, and So On
Refreshments

Program Covers — Use sponge painting to decorate your front
covers. Cut 3-toed dinosaur footprints from sponges. Let the children
dip them in shallow dishes of tempera paint and print over all of the
front covers.

PREPARATION

Children's Planning:

- Enjoy a unit about dinosaurs with the children.

- Discuss several types of dinosaurs so the children know one or two facts about each one.

ANKYLOSAURUS: (ank-eye-loh-SAW-rus) Means curved lizard. It had bones all over its body with a large bone at the end of its tail that was used as a weapon. It ate low plants and bushes.

BRACHIOSAURUS: (brack-ee-oh-SAW-russ) This may have been one of the biggest land animals that ever lived. It weighed as much as twelve elephants. The front legs were longer than the back so it stood like a giraffe with a sloping back. It stayed close to water.

BRONTOSAURUS: (brahnt-e-SAWR-as) This dinosaur was a biggie too. It was called the 'thunder lizard.' It lived in the water and ate plants.

PTERODACTYL: (tehr-a-DAK-til) It had wings but no tail, teeth, or feathers. It couldn't walk well or fly well either. It took off from tall trees and cliffs and glided for miles looking to spear fish for food.

STEGOSAURUS: (STEG-e-SAWR-es) This one is called the 'roofed lizard.' This small headed dinosaur had a brain the size of a walnut in its head. It had a larger brain near its hips to control its back legs and tail. It had plates down its back for protection. It ate plants.

TRICERATOPS: (TRI-SER-e-tops) This word means 'three horned face.' It was a plant eater which weighed about as much as five small cars. Its huge head was about one third as long as its body.

TYRANNOSAURUS REX: (ty-ran-e-SAWR-es rex) This dinosaur name means 'tyrant-lizard king.' He was the largest and meanest of the meat eaters. Tyrannosaurus could run very fast on his back legs but his front legs were small and weak.

- Give the children opportunities to tell each other about dinosaurs.

- At the end of the unit let each child choose his favorite dinosaur.

Classroom Preparation:

- Make the stations so the children can use them in the classroom during the unit. (See Set-up section.)

- The children should make pictures or models of their favorite dinosaurs which will be shown to the group during the program. They may be painted, drawn with crayon, chalk or marker, or constructed with soft dough. Some children might want to glue or staple small objects together such as paper rolls, styrofoam pieces, cloth, wire, etc. onto a base to represent a dinosaur.

- Review the rhymes and songs.

Songs and Fingerplays:

- *All About Dinosaurs*
- *I'm Bringing Home a Baby Dinosaur*
- *The Ill-Mannered Dinosaur*

Costumes: Any hat or visor with a brim brought from home.

Nametags: Dinosaur footprint

Decorations: Have a display of commercial or handmade dinosaur models set-up on your tables. Have a fossil collection displayed on another table.

Set-up:

- You'll need a recording of Prokofiev's, 'Peter and the Wolf.'

- Write children's names on masking tape and put them on the floor where the children should stand after walking in.

- The stations should be set around the room with necessary materials so that all of the people can participate at each station during the program. Have a large paper dinosaur footprint to mark each station. Write the name of each activity and the directions on the footprint.

STATION 1 — Make the game board for the 'Dinosaur Trail.' Draw 24 dinosaur footprints in a maze around a piece of tagboard. Have dinosaur stickers interspersed among the footprints. You'll also need a die or a spinner (1-6) and rubber dinosaurs (or other small objects) to use as markers.

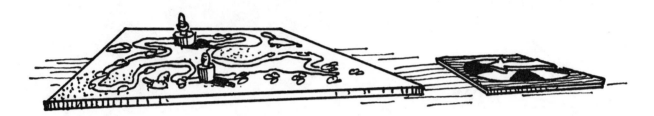

STATION 2 — Have four or five dinosaur books for the adults and children to read together. Here are a few titles, *Terrible Tyrannosaurus* by Elizabeth Charlton; *Time of the Dinosaurs* by Ann and Stafford Packard and Shirley Stafford; *Digging of Dinosaurs* by Aliki; *My Visit To the Dinosaurs* by Aliki; *Dinosaur Alphabet Book* by Patricia Whitehead.

STATION 3 — Gather several dinosaur puzzles or make them by gluing dinosaur pictures on pieces of posterboard, covering them with clear Contact® paper, and then cutting them into pieces.

STATION 4 — Mix a batch of Baker's Clay ahead of time to make fossils. Have a box of textured objects such as shells, leaves, etc.

Baker's Clay
(no cook recipe)

You'll Need:
2 cups flour
1 cup salt
½ cup water
2 Tbs vegetable oil

To Make: Combine the flour and salt in a large flat-bottomed bowl. Add the water slowly. Mix as you pour. Form into a ball. Note: Additional water may be necessary depending on the humidity. Take care not to add too much or the dough will become sticky. Knead the dough for 7-10 minutes until it is smooth and firm. Store in a plastic bag.

STATION 5 — Make the cards for 'Dinosaur Sort.' Purchase a package of dinosaur stickers and zoo or farm animal stickers. Cut pieces of posterboard into 3"x4" pieces and put one sticker on each card. Cover each with clear Contact®. Get two paperplates. Mark one 'long ago' and the other 'today.'

STATION 6 — 'Shape a Dinosaur.' Have soft dough available for the people to model into dinosaurs.

Soft Dough

You'll Need:
4 cups of flour
1 cup salt
4 Tbs alum
2 Tbs vegetable oil
3 cups of boiling water
 (Add drops of food
 coloring to the water.)

To Make: Mix the first four ingredients together in a large bowl. Add the boiling water and stir until the dough is cool, knead by hand. Turn the dough on the table and continue kneading until it is thoroughly mixed.

STATION 7 — Cut a large piece of butcher paper for a mural. Draw dinosaur shapes on thick sponges and cut them out. Pour paint into shallow pans.

STATION 8 — Get a dinosaur filmstrip and projector from your local library. Have a screen readily available. Instead of a filmstrip, you might want to show the video, *Mr. Rogers, Dinosaurs and Monsters*, Family Communications, Inc. 1986.

Refreshments: Fossil Cookies, Dinosaur Bones, and Juice.

Fossil Cookies

You'll Need:
1 box yellow cake mix
½ cup softened butter
½ cup vegetable oil
2 Tbs water
2 eggs

To Make: Mix all of the ingredients well. Roll the dough into balls. Place on an ungreased cookie sheet. Flatten each ball with a fork to form fossil criss-cross pattern. Bake at 350° for 12-15 minutes.

Dinosaur Bones

You'll Need:
1 stick margarine
2 cups Wheat Chex
2 cups Rice Chex
2 cups Corn Chex
1 cup mixed nuts
2 cups pretzels
1 tsp seasoning salt
2 tsp Worcestershire sauce

To Make: Preheat your oven to 250°. Melt butter in 15"x10"x2" pan. Remove the pan from the oven. Stir in seasoning salt and Worchestershire sauce. Add cereal, nuts, and pretzels. Mix to coat. Bake 1 hour, stirring frequently. Spread on absorbent paper to cool.

PRESENTATION

Children lumber in wearing their hats or visors to the music of 'Peter and the Wolf.' They go to the front of the room and stand there while being introduced.

TEACHER: "Ladies and gentlemen, thank you for joining us. I would like to introduce you to our scientists and archeologists." (Introduce the children by name.)

NARRATOR: "Today they have come to teach you about the great and small dinosaurs that roamed the earth long ago. Listen carefully to their song."

ALL ABOUT DINOSAURS
(tune: Mary Had a Little Lamb)

Dinosaurs lived a long time ago,
A long time ago, a long time ago.
Dinosaurs lived a long time ago,
Their bones were left behind.

The Tyrannosaurous was a mean ol' thing,
A mean ol' thing, a mean ol' thing.
The Tyrannosaurous was a mean ol' thing,
'Cause he ate all the others.

The Stegosaurus was all bumpy,
Was all bumpy, was all bumpy.
The Stegosaurus was all bumpy,
And he had two brains.

The Brachiosaurous lived in the water,
Lived in the water, lived in the water.
The Brachiosaurous lived in the water,
Because he only ate plants.

The Trachodon had 2000 teeth,
2000 teeth, 2000 teeth.
The Trachodon had 2000 teeth,
So he was called rough-toothed.

The Ankylosaurous' back was curved,
Back was curved, back was curved.
The Ankylosaurous' back was curved,
That's how he got his name.

The Brontosaurous was very big,
Very big, very big.
The Brontosaurous was very big,
He lived on plants and leaves.

The Pterodactyl was the winged flier,
Was the winged flier, was the winged flier.
The Pterodactyl was the winged flier,
But he didn't have any feathers.

Tricerotops had three horns,
Three horns, three horns.
Tricerotops had three horns,
That's how he got his name.

Now you know all about dinosaurs,
About dinosaurs, about dinosaurs.
Now you know all about dinosaurs,
So our song is through.

by Valerie Bielsker

114

NARRATOR: "As you learned in this song, there were many types of dinosaurs. The children are going to show you the models or pictures they have made of their favorite dinosaurs and tell you a little more about each one." (Children are called forward two or three at a time to show the model, picture, or what they have made about one particular type of dinosaur. They can each tell about their dinosaur. It can be as simple as naming the dinosaur or more detailed by describing its characteristics.)

NARRATOR: "Scientists and archeologists study the bones and fossils of the dinosaurs to determine their size and shape. Have you ever thought of having your very own dinosaur? Our next song is about just that."

I'M BRINGING HOME A BABY DINOSAUR

I'm bringing home a baby dinosaur
Won't my mother fall right through the floor?
I'm bringing home a baby dinosaur
Oh, he's squishing me.

I'm tying up my baby dinosaur
Won't my mother fall right through the floor?
I'm tying up my baby dinosaur
Now it will be mine forever more.

by Susan Spaete

NARRATOR: "Now that you have a dinosaur living with you, you might want to know what and how it eats. The children will tell you."

THE ILL-MANNERED DINOSAUR

Never go to lunch with a dinosaur,
They're a mean, foul, nasty group.
They burp and slurp and never sit down,
They're likely to step in your soup.

The biggest are called vegetarians,
Which means they eat grass and trees.
But when you're longer than a school bus,
You can eat whatever you please.

The rest are called carnivores,
Which means they eat mostly meat.
If there aren't enough hot dogs to go around,
They'll probably chomp on your feet.

And when it comes time to clear the plates,
They'll try to sneak away.
Instead of helping with dishes,
They'll want to go out to play.

by Dick Wilmes

NARRATOR: "Now our young scientists and archeologists will go to the stations which have been set-up around the room. You are invited to join them and take part in each activity."

STATION 1 — Play 'Dinosaur Trail.' Roll the dice or flick the spinner and move that many spaces along the Dinosaur Trail. If a player lands on a dinosaur instead of a footprint, he misses his next turn. The game is over when everyone has reached the end of the Trail.

STATION 2 — Enjoy reading a book together.

STATION 3 — Choose a puzzle of your favorite dinosaur and see if you can put all of its pieces together.

STATION 4 — Make a fossil by rolling out a small piece of the clay and then making an imprint in it with a leaf, shell, or other object. Take it home and let it harden. Paint it if you'd like.

STATION 5 — 'Dinosaur Sort.' Mix up all of the cards. Have two plates, one marked 'long ago' and the other one marked 'today.' Look at each card and decide which pile it should go on. Continue until all of the cards have been sorted.

STATION 6 — 'Shape a Dinosaur.' Using the soft dough, design and shape your favorite dinosaur.

STATION 7 — Dinosaur Mural. Have the paper, sponge shapes, and paint on the table. Let everyone print several dinosaur shapes. When it has dried, hang it up.

STATION 8 — Get comfortable and enjoy a film about dinosaurs.

NARRATOR: "When you have finished, join us in a snack of Dinosaur Bones, Fossil Cookies and Juice."

A VISIT TO THE FARM

Teacher	Welcome
Children Enter	*Walk in to the music of 'Farmer in the Dell'*
Song	*Old McChild's Name Had a Farm*
Song	*B I N G O*
Fingerplay	*The Barnyard Gate*
Poem	*Baa Baa Black Sheep*
Song	*Five Little Ducks*
Drama	The Little Red Hen
Special Guest	
Refreshments	

Program Covers — Fold the two outer edges of a piece of red construction paper to meet in the center. Cut away the top to form the barn roof. Glue white paper doors and windows to the front. The children can draw animals on the inside. Open the doors and put the program information on the inside of the barn.

117

PREPARATION

Children's Planning:

- Take a field trip to a nearby farm.

- Let each child choose what animal he'd like to be for the program.

- Read the story of the 'Little Red Hen.'

Classroom Preparation:

- Review the rhymes, songs, and fingerplays.

- Practice pantomiming 'The Little Red Hen.'

Songs and Fingerplays:

- *The Farmer In the Dell*
- *Old McDonald Had a Farm*
- *B I N G O*
- *The Barnyard Gate*
- *Baa Baa Black Sheep*
- *Five Little Ducks*

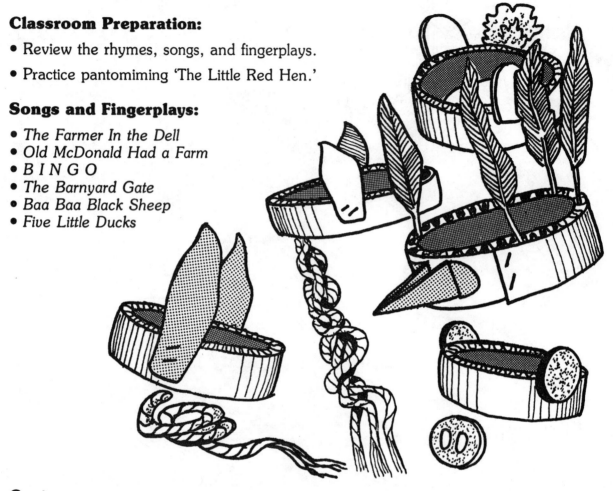

Costumes:

- One or more children can dress as a farmer.

- The children may wear clothes the color of the animal they have chosen, for example a white shirt and pants for the sheep.

- If the children choose to make animal headbands, cut strips about two inches wide from corrugated cardboard. Add animal features to the bands to depict each animal. Staple or tape them to fit the children's heads. Add other features if the children would like.

CHICKEN and DUCK: Stick feathers into the corrugation of the band, cut a construction paper beak or bill, and attach it to the front.

HORSE: Add ears to the band. Use yarn for the tail. Tuck it into the child's waist.

COW· Add ears to the band. Using three 20″ pieces of yarn, braid them ¾ of the way down. Leave the bottom bushy. Tuck the tail into the child's waist. Cut construction paper dots for the spots and tape them to the child's clothes.

PIG: Attach pink ears to the band. Cut a circle out of construction paper and draw two dots on it. Tape it to the child's nose. Coil a pipe cleaner for the tail.

SHEEP: Add ears and cotton to the band. Wad up a six inch piece of white paper. Glue cotton to it and use for a tail.

DOG: Add ears to the band. Tail may vary.

Nametags: Barn-shape

Decorations: None

Set-up:

- Using large blocks build the pens for the 'animals.' Remember to leave openings in each one so the 'animals' can easily get in and out of their pens. Put the children's mats into each pen.

- You'll need a recording of the 'Farmer In the Dell.'

- Invite a farmer, 4-H representative, or other area person familiar with farming to speak to the group about farms. You might also want to arrange for him/her to be the narrator for 'The Little Red Hen' if you decide to include it in the program.

Refreshments: Deviled Eggs, Fresh Bread or Buns, Child-Made Butter, and Milk.

Deviled Eggs

You'll Need:
6 hard-boiled eggs
3 Tbs salad dressing
1 Tbs prepared mustard

To Make: Shell the eggs. Cut them in half length-wise. Slip out the yolks & mash them with a fork. Mix in salad dressing to moisten. Add the mustard. Carefully spoon the yolk mixture back into the whites. Cover and refrigerate until ready to serve.

Butter

You'll Need:
1 pint whipping cream
1 qt jar with tight lid

To Make: Pour whipping cream into the jar. Secure the cover. Let the children shake the jar until butter is formed and separates from the liquid. Strain the liquid off. Squeeze the excess liquid out of the butter. Strain it off. Serve with fresh bread.

PRESENTATION

TEACHER: "Our visit to the farm was so much fun that we have decided to bring the farm back to school. Thank you for joining us." (The farmer enters as the first verse of 'Farmer In the Dell' is sung by the audience or played from a recording. The next verse is sung and that animal comes and stands next to the farmer, etc.)

THE FARMER IN THE DELL

The farmer in the dell, the farmer in the dell
Hi, ho the dairy oh, the farmer in the dell.

The farmer brought his dog, the farmer brought his dog
Hi, ho the dairy oh, the farmer brought his dog.

The farmer brought his horse, cows, pigs, sheep, ducks, chicken, etc.
(When all are together the first verse is sung again.)

NARRATOR: "Let's meet our farmer (or farmers) and the animals. The best way to do this is through our next song. 'Old Mc**Child's Name** Had a Farm'."

OLD MC(CHILD'S NAME) HAD A FARM

*Old Mc***Child's Name** *had a farm, ee, i, ee, i, o*
And on his/her farm he/she had a dog, ee, i, ee, i, o.
With an arf, arf here and an arf, arf there
Here an arf, there an arf, everywhere an arf, arf.
*Old Mc***Child's Name** *had a farm, ee, i, ee, i, o.*
(Child pretending to be the dog sings the 'Arf' sounds. Continue the song with the animals singing their parts.)

120

NARRATOR: "We had better put our animals in their pens. (Animals go into the pens, the farmer and the dog do not.) Farmer Mc**Child's Name,** I see you have a friendly dog. What is his name?" (All of the children sing.)

BINGO

There was a farmer had a dog, and Bingo was his name Oh,
B I N G O,   B I N G O,   B I N G O, and Bingo was his name Oh!

There was a farmer had a dog, and Bingo was his name Oh,
B I N G (Clap), *B I N G* (Clap), *B I N G* (Clap), *and Bingo was his name Oh!*

There was a farmer had a dog, and Bingo was his name Oh,
B I N (Clap twice), *B I N* (clap twice), *B I N* (clap twice), *and Bingo was his name Oh!*

There was a farmer had a dog, and Bingo was his name Oh,
B I (clap 3 times), *B I* (clap 3 times), *B I* (clap 3 times), *and Bingo was his name Oh!*

There was a farmer had a dog, and Bingo was his name Oh,
B (clap 4 times), *B* (clap 4 times), *B* (clap 4 times), *and Bingo was his name Oh!*

There was a farmer had a dog, and Bingo was his name Oh,
(clap 5 times), (clap 5 times), (clap 5 times), *and Bingo was his name OHHHHH!*

NARRATOR: "Farmer Mc**Child's Name** may we tour your farm? I see here in the first pen you have horses and cows." (The children in these pens stand, recite the rhyme, and then sit down.)

THE BARNYARD GATE

I have a little horse by the barnyard gate
And that little horse is my playmate.
That little horse says, "Neigh, neigh, neigh, neigh."
(Horses say "Neigh.")

I have a little cow by the barnyard gate
And that little cow is my playmate.
That little cow says "Moo, moo, moo, moo."
(Cows say 'Moo.")

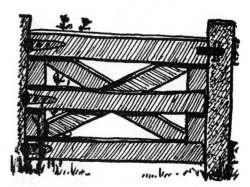

121

NARRATOR: "What is in this pen? Oh, look at these cute pigs and then some chickens." (These children stand, recite the rhyme, and then sit down.)

> I have a little pig by the barnyard gate
> And that little pig is my playmate.
> That little pig says, "Oink, oink, oink."
> (Pigs say "Oink.")
>
> I have a little chicken by the barnyard gate
> And that little chicken is my playmate.
> That little chicken says, "Cluck! Cluck! Cluck!"
> (Chickens say "Cluck.")

NARRATOR: "Look at these woolly sheep. Do you get much wool from them?" (Children who are sheep sing.)

BAA BAA BLACK SHEEP

> Baa, baa black sheep have you any wool?
> Yes sir, yes sir, three bags full.
> One for my master and one for my dame
> And none for the little boy who cries in the lane.

NARRATOR: "How many ducks do you have? Let's count them?" (Children who are ducks can say this rhyme.)

FIVE LITTLE DUCKS

> Five little ducks that I once knew,
> Fat one, skinny one, fair ones two
> But the one little duck with the feather on his back
> (Put hands on back waist and wave them)
> He led the others with a "Quack, quack, quack,
> Quack, quack, quack; quack, quack, quack."
> He led the others with a "Quack, quack, quack."
>
> Down to the river they would go,
> Wibble-wobble, wibble-wobble, to and fro (Sway back and forth)
> But the one little duck with the feather on his back
> (Put hands on back waist and wave them)
> He led the others with a "Quack, quack, quack,
> Quack, quack, quack; quack, quack, quack."
> He led the others with a "Quack, quack, quack!"

THE LITTLE RED HEN

(Optional: Dramatic play of the 'Little Red Hen.' All of the animals are used as they are. The Little Red Hen is one of the chickens. The children may speak the animal parts or pantomime as the narrator tells the story. You might ask your special guest to be the narrator for the play. Be sure to have this prepared ahead of time.)

NARRATOR: "I want to thank Farmer Mc**Child's Name** for the excellent tour. You have some remarkable animals on your farm. Thank you." (Children bow and sit down. Introduce the special guest.)

NARRATOR: "Thank you for sharing our excitement about the farm. Farmer Mc**Child's Name** and his animal friends have prepared a real farm snack. All of you — parents, friends, brothers, sisters, and our special guest, please join us for Deviled Eggs, Homemade Butter, Fresh Buns, and Cold Milk."

SPRING IS IN THE AIR

Children Enter	Walking in With Umbrellas
Dance	*Rain, Rain Go Away*
Teacher	Welcome
Song	*Rain, Rain Go Away*
Activity	*The Flower Garden*
Rhyme	*Planting*
Rhyme	*Pussy Willow*
Fingerplay	*Robin With a Yellow Bill*
Song	*Glunk, Glunk*
Song	*Five Little Ducks*
Refreshments	

Program Covers — Fold construction paper in half for the programs. Make umbrellas for the front of each program by cutting paper doilies in half and gluing them on the construction paper. Cut pipe cleaners in half, bend one end for a handle and glue it to the bottom of the doily. Add rain by dotting the paper with glue and sprinkling glitter on each dot. Shake off the excess glitter.

PREPARATION

Children's Planning:

- Discuss the various signs of Spring.

- Enjoy several Springtime walks. Look for flowers, baby animals, worms, etc.

- Talk about the growth of flowers and plants.

Classroom Preparation:

- Learn the 'Umbrella Dance.' The children should hold their umbrellas over their heads and spin them to the count of four. They should continue the dance by:

  1. Spinning their umbrellas in front of them to the count of four,
  2. Spinning them to the side to the count of four,
  3. Spinning them to the other side to the count of four and then overhead again. Repeat the sequence until the music has ended.

- Practice pantomime and dance for 'The Flower Garden.'

- Review the rhymes and songs.

Songs and Fingerplays:

- *Rain, Rain Go Away*
- *The Flower Garden*
- *Planting*
- *Pussy Willow*
- *Robin With a Yellow Bill*
- *Glunk, Glunk*
- *Five Little Ducks*

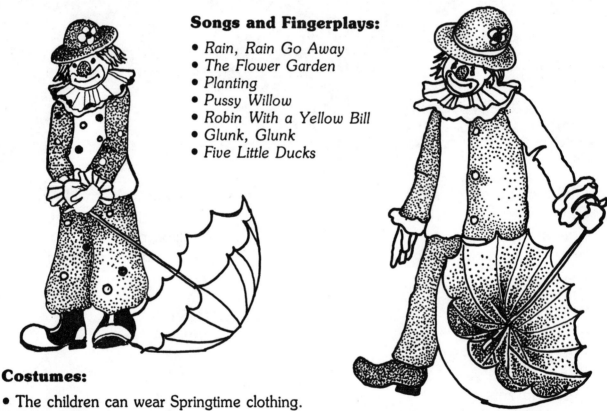

Costumes:

- The children can wear Springtime clothing.

- Each child needs a child-size umbrella.

- Each child can make a flower collar to wear during the rhyme, 'The Flower Garden.' To make, pre-cut collar shapes from construction paper and let the children glue on flower shapes cut from pieces of pastel colored tissue paper.

- The farmer needs a straw hat and the fairy needs a wand made from a dowel rod covered with foil and wings cut from construction paper.

- Make a large sun from yellow posterboard.

Nametags: Flower

Decorations:

- Fresh flowers or plants when appropriate. (Maybe you could have a plant for each family. They could take them home and plant them outside for the summer.)

- Buy tissue paper bells of bright colors. (These can be found in card stores). Turn them upside-down to form tulips. Attach narrow dowel rods to the bottoms of the bells to form the stems for free standing tulips. (Variation: Half-opened bells can be placed upside-down on the bulletin board to form tulips. The leaves can be made by using construction paper glued to the stem.)

Set-up:

- Put the children's mats or strips of tape with their names on them where the children are to stand during the 'Umbrella Dance.' Make sure there is ample room between children.

- You'll need a recording of 'Rain, Rain Go Away.'

- Arrange for an adult to help the children put on their flower collars before 'The Flower Garden.'

- Place the props for the 'flower activity' in a convenient place.

- You'll need a recording of the 'Dance of the Flowers' from the Nutcracker Suite.

Refreshments: Fruit Sandwiches or Hard Boiled Egg Flowers with a Glass of Juice.

Fruit Sandwiches

You'll Need:
   esh fruit such as:
   bananas
   strawberries
   grapes
Vanilla pudding
Vanilla wafers

To Make: Clean and cut the fruit into bite-size pieces. Prepare vanilla pudding according to your favorite recipe. Put a small amount of pudding on each wafer and top with a piece of fruit.

Egg Flowers

You'll Need:
Hard boiled eggs
Radishes
Celery sticks

To Make: Peel the hard boiled eggs. Cut them into circle slices. Place the egg circles around radish slices. Add celery stick stems.

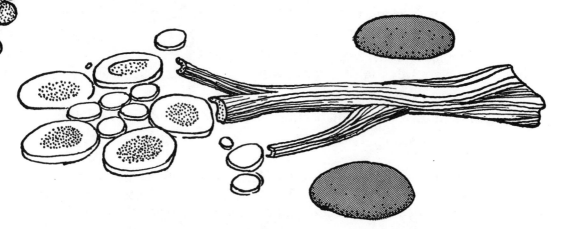

PRESENTATION

Children walk to their assigned places with umbrellas resting on their shoulders. When the music, 'Rain, Rain Go Away' begins, the children hold their umbrellas over their heads and spin them to the count of four. They continue the 'Umbrella Dance' until the music stops.

Teacher welcomes everyone to the Springtime Program.

NARRATOR: "Enjoy listening as the children sing, 'Rain, Rain Go Away' to open our program." (Children should hold their umbrellas over their shoulders as they sing.)

RAIN, RAIN GO AWAY

It's raining, it's pouring,
The old man is snoring,
He bumped his head and he went to bed
And he didn't get up in the morning.
Rain, rain go away
Come again some other day.

(The children should sit on their mats after singing and someone should collect the umbrellas.)

NARRATOR: "Look, the rain has gone away and the sun is coming out. Watch what is going to happen now." (An adult places the collars on the children who will blossom into flowers. They should curl up into a ball. In addition one child holds up the sun, one is the fairy with the wand and wings, and another child is the farmer wearing the straw hat. The narrator slowly reads the rhyme as the children pantomime.)

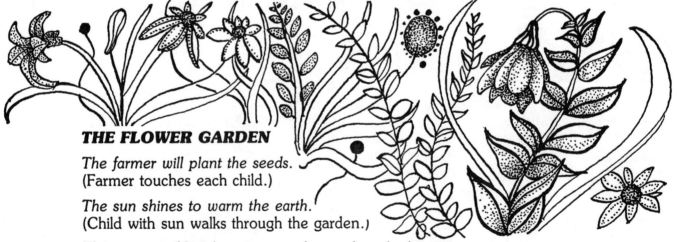

THE FLOWER GARDEN

The farmer will plant the seeds.
(Farmer touches each child.)

The sun shines to warm the earth.
(Child with sun walks through the garden.)

The rain sprinkles down to give the seeds a drink.
(Rain fairy tiptoes through the garden and touches each seed with her wand.)

The flowers begin to grow.
(The seeds lift their heads, then arms, kneel, then stand and stretch.)

Until we have a beautiful garden.

(Play 'Dance of the Flowers' from the Nutcracker Suite in the background as the children quietly dance around the stage. After the music has stopped, the children come back to the center and say the next flower rhyme.)

PLANTING

I took a little seed one day
About a month ago.
I put it in a pot of dirt,
In hopes that it would grow.

I poured a little water
To make the soil right.
I set the pot upon the sill,
Where the sun would give it light.

I checked the pot most every day,
And turned it once or twice.
With a little care and water
I helped it grow so nice.

by Dick Wilmes

NARRATOR: "Flowers aren't the only things that let us know that Spring is here. Sometimes before the flowers come we see pussy willows blooming. Listen as the children tell you about the fuzzy plant." (The children can remain in the center while saying this rhyme.)

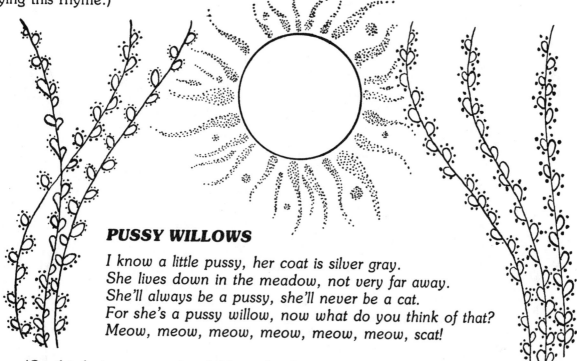

PUSSY WILLOWS

I know a little pussy, her coat is silver gray.
She lives down in the meadow, not very far away.
She'll always be a pussy, she'll never be a cat.
For she's a pussy willow, now what do you think of that?
Meow, meow, meow, meow, meow, meow, scat!

(On this last sentence the children should bend down and gradually stand as they say "Meow." When they say "Scat" they should jump up and spread their arms apart as if shooing the cat away.)

NARRATOR: "We always look for the first robin to come back from the south to tell us that Spring is really here."

ROBIN WITH A YELLOW BILL

Robin with a yellow bill,
Hopped upon my window sill.
Cocked his shiny eye and said,
"Aren't you ashamed, you sleepy head."

127

NARRATOR: "If we are able to take a walk in the country on a spring evening we would recognize the chirp of the frogs. Our children will sing a song about a frog for you."

GLUNK, GLUNK

Glunk, glunk went the little green frog one day
Glunk, glunk went the little green frog,
Glunk, glunk went the little green frog one day
And the frog went, glunk, glunk, glunk!

(Make the "glunk" sound by flipping your tongue in back of your mouth.)

NARRATOR: "The animals have their young in the Spring. We just love to see a mother duck with her ducklings all in a row. Listen to the children tell you about 'Five Little Ducks' that they know."

FIVE LITTLE DUCKS

Five little ducks that I once knew,
Fat one skinny one, fair ones two,
But the one little duck with the feather on his back
He led the others with a "Quack, quack, quack,
Quack, quack, quack; quack, quack, quack."
He led the others with a "Quack, quack, quack."

Down to the river they would go,
Wibble-wobble, wibble-wobble, to and fro,
But the one little duck with the feather on his back
He led the others with a "Quack, quack, quack,
Quack, quack, quack; quack, quack, quack."
He led the others with a "Quack, quack, quack!"

Back from the river they did come,
Wibble-wobble, wibble-wobble, ho-ho-hum,
But the one little duck with the feather on his back
He led the others with a "Quack, quack, quack,
Quack, quack, quack; quack, quack, quack."
He led the others with a "Quack, quack, quack!"

NARRATOR: "Thank you for coming on this Spring day. Please join us for a Glass of Juice, some Egg Flowers, or a Fruit Sandwich which the children have prepared."

FOR EVERYTHING THERE'S A SEASON

Children Enter	Children slowly run to their places
Teacher	Welcome
Dance	Ribbon Dance
Rhyme	*Welcome*
Fingerplay	*Five Little Jack-O-Lanterns*
Fingerplay	*Gobble, Gobble, Gobble*
Song	*Jingle Bells*
Fingerplay	*Five Little Valentines*
Song	*Five Little Ducks*
Rhyme	*I Stuck My Head In A Little Skunk's Hole*
Rhyme	*Beehive*
Song	*Yankee Doodle Dandy*
Guest	
Refreshments	

Program Covers — Fold construction paper in half to form the programs. Have the children collage seasonal shapes on the covers. Insert a list of all of the children in the class inside of the programs.

129

PREPARATION

Children's Planning:

- Talk with the children about all of the activities they remember doing during the Autumn, Winter, Spring, and Summer. Write down what they say.

- Have each child choose which season he liked best and what he liked to do in that season.

- Remind them of their favorite songs, rhymes, and games from each season.

Classroom Preparations:

- Review the rhymes, songs, and dances the children liked from each season. Use rhythm sticks while singing 'Yankee Doodle Dandy'.

- Have each child paint a picture at the easel of something he liked about his favorite season. When each child is done, have him tell you about his picture. You write what he says on the back or bottom of his picture. Save all of the art.

- Teach the children the Ribbon Dance using 'Move, Move, Move' by Fred Koch from the album *This Lil' Cow*. They should shake, push, and jump the sticks according to the directions on the record. (Younger children may want to only move their sticks up and down or side to side to the beat of the music.)

Songs and Fingerplays:

- *Welcome*
- *Five Little Jack-O-Lanterns*
- *Gobble, Gobble, Gobble*
- *Jingle Bells*
- *Five Little Valentines*
- *Five Little Ducks*
- *I Stuck My Head In a Little Skunk's Hole*
- *Beehive*
- *Yankee Doodle Dandy*

Costumes:

- Autumn — jeans and sweater or sweatshirt
- Winter — hat and scarf
- Spring — dress clothes
- Summer — shorts, sunglasses, visors

Nametags: Leaves, snowflakes, flowers, and suns

Decorations: Place natural flowers, leaves, and evergreen boughs on the tables.

Set-Up:

- Put the children's mats in place.
- Put strips of masking tape on the floor to show the children where they stand while discussing the pictures they painted.
- You'll need a record player and a copy of the album *This Lil' Cow* by Fred Koch for the Ribbon Dance.
- Make (buy) ribbon sticks for all of the children. Use half inch dowel rods cut in one foot pieces. Tie colorful ribbons to one end of each stick.
- Have the children's paintings under their mats.
- Have the rhythm instruments readily available to pass out to the children just before they sing 'Yankee Doodle Dandy.'
- Invite a clown or juggler to entertain and talk with the children.

Refreshments: Juice Popsicles and several kinds of cool drinks.

Popsicles

You'll Need:
Variety of juices
Popsicle sticks
Small paper cups

To Make: Fill each cup about 3/4 full of juice. Put the cups on a tray and slide into the freezer. When the juice is partially frozen, insert the popsicle sticks. Let them freeze.

Children enter holding their ribbon sticks high in the air as they slowly run to their mats.

TEACHER: "Welcome everyone to our end-of-the-year program. The children would like to begin by showing you how they can move and twirl their ribbon sticks in the Ribbon Dance." (The children stand and as soon as the music begins they dance. After the dance all of the children stand on their mats.)

NARRATOR: "The children are really happy you all came. Listen as they say their 'Welcome' rhyme for you."

WELCOME

Welcome to our classroom
(Stretch arms out as if welcoming everyone.)
Where we started school last fall
_____ little children
Not all quite so tall. (Put a hand on top of head.)

We've learned many good things
As we came to school each day
And now we will share them with you
So listen as we say. (Hold hands behind ears.)
(All of the children sit down.)

NARRATOR: "These children (name the children) liked Autumn the best. They have painted pictures to help them tell you what some of their favorite things were." (The children who like Autumn the best pick up their paintings and walk to the masking tape. One at a time the children should hold up their paintings and tell everyone about them or they should ask an adult to read what is written on the paintings. After all of the Autumn children have told about their paintings they should move back to their mats and stand. The other children stand.)

NARRATOR: "One of our favorite rhymes in the Autumn was 'Five Little Jack-O-Lanterns'."

FIVE LITTLE JACK-O-LANTERNS

Five little jack-o-lanterns were sitting on a gate.
The first one said, "My, it's getting late."
The second one said, "I hear a noise."
The third one said, "It's only some boys."
The fourth one said, "Come on let's run."
The fifth one said, "It's Halloween fun."
Poof went the wind.
Out went the lights.
Away ran the Jack-O-Lanterns on Halloween night.

NARRATOR: "At Thanksgiving we enjoyed many turkey rhymes. Our favorite one was 'Gobble, Gobble, Gobble'."

GOBBLE, GOBBLE, GOBBLE

The turkey is a funny bird.
His head goes wobble, wobble. (Shake head up and down.)
But all he says is just one word, (Hold up one finger.)
"Gobble, gobble, gobble."
(All of the children sit down. The Winter children pick up their paintings and move to their strips of masking tape.)

NARRATOR: "These children (name the children) liked Winter the best. They have painted pictures to tell you about their favorite activities." (As with the Autumn children, let these children tell everyone about their paintings. When finished they should move back to their mats and stand with the other children while saying the rhymes.)

NARRATOR: "Our favorite Winter song was 'Jingle Bells'. Please join us as we sing."

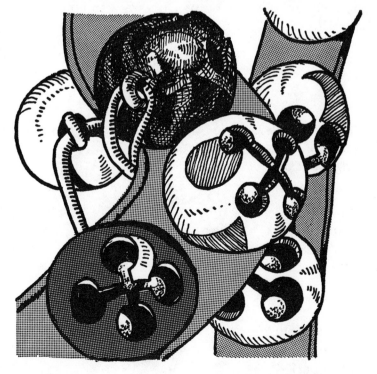

JINGLE BELLS

Jingle bells, jingle bells,
Jingle all the way.
Oh, what fun it is to ride
In a one horse open sleigh. Hey!

Dashing through the snow,
In a one horse open sleigh,
O'er the fields we go
Laughing all the way.

Bells on bobtails ring
Making spirits bright
What fun it is to ride and sing
A sleighing song tonight.

Jingle bells, jingle bells,
Jingle all the way.
Oh, what fun it is to ride
In a one horse open sleigh. Hey!

NARRATOR: "Listen to the children talk about five of their favorite Valentines."

FIVE LITTLE VALENTINES

Five little valentines were having a race.
The first one was frilly with lace.
The second one had a funny face.
The third one said, "I love you."
The fourth one said, "I do too."
The fifth one was sly as a fox.
He ran the fastest to your Valentine Box.
(All of the children should sit down and the Spring children should pick up their paintings and move to the masking tape.)

NARRATOR: "These children (name them) liked Spring the best. Listen as they show and tell you why." (The Spring children should hold up their paintings and tell everyone about them or have someone read their dictation. When they have finished, the children should move back to their mats and stand with the rest of the children.)

NARRATOR: "Spring is a time when many baby animals are born. Ducks are so cute. The children have a rhyme about 'Five Little Ducks'."

FIVE LITTLE DUCKS

Five little ducks that I once knew,
Fat one, skinny one, fair ones two,
But the one little duck with the feather on his back,
He led the others with a "Quack, quack, quack!"
He led the others with a "Quack, quack, quack!"

Down to the river they did go.
Wibble-wobble, wibble-wobble to and fro.
But the one little duck with the feather on his back,
He led the others with a "Quack, quack, quack!"
He led the others with a "Quack, quack, quack!"

Back from the river they did come,
Wibble-wobble, wibble-wobble ho, ho, hum,
But the one little duck with the feather on his back,
He led the others with a "Quack, quack, quack!"
He led the others with a "Quack, quack, quack!"

134

NARRATOR: "Listen to the children tell you what happens when they explore a skunk's hole."

I STUCK MY HEAD IN A LITTLE SKUNK'S HOLE

I stuck my head in a little skunk's hole,
And the little skunk said "Why bless my soul,
Take it out, take it out, take it out,
Remove it."

I didn't take it out and the little skunk said,
"You'd better take it out or you'll wish you had.
Take it out, take it out, take it out.
Pssssss!" (Make spraying sound)
I removed it too late. (Hold noses.)
(All of the children sit down and the Summer children move to the masking tape.)

NARRATOR: "These children (name them) like the warm, sunny days of Summer the best. Enjoy what they say." (The Summer children should hold up their paintings and tell about them. When finished they should move back to their mats. All of the children stand.)

NARRATOR: "Summer is a time of picnics, parades, and flags. The children want to tell you about one picnic pest they do not like — the bee."

BEEHIVE

Here is the beehive (Hold up fist.)
Where are the bees? (Look around.)
Hidden away where nobody sees.
Soon they come creeping out of the hive.
One, two, three, four, five. (Hold up fingers while counting.)

NARRATOR: "Our children are going to sing 'Yankee Doodle Dandy' as they play their rhythm instruments. Join them in this last song by singing and clapping along. (Pass out the rhythm instruments.)

YANKEE DOODLE DANDY

Yankee Doodle went to town
A riding on a pony.
Stuck a feather in his cap
And called it macaroni.

Yankee Doodle keep it up.
Yankee Doodle Dandy
Mind the music and the step
And with the girls be handy.

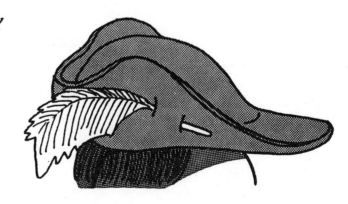

NARRATOR: "Today we have a very special visitor." (Introduce the guest.)

NARRATOR: "Thank you for coming. Please join us for some cool refreshments."

WHEN I GROW UP

Children Enter . . . . Marching to Music
Teacher . . . . Welcome
Song . . . . *When I Grow Up*
Astronaut . . . . *One Is For The Rocket*
Bus Driver . . . . *Wheels On The Bus*
Dancers . . . . *Scarf Dance*
Firefighter . . . . *The Firefighters*
Juggler . . . . Ball Skills
Musician . . . . *Rhythm Band*
Police . . . . *Five Little Police Officers*
Teacher . . . . *ABC Song*
Zookeeper . . . . *Mr. Alligator*
Refreshments

Program Covers — Have the children cut pictures of grown-ups from magazines and collage them on the fronts of each program.

PREPARATION

Children's Planning:

- Have a unit at the end of the year focusing on occupations.

- Have the children choose their favorite occupations.

- Tell the children that at their last program of the year, they can tell everyone what they'd like to be when they grow up.

- If children know, have them choose songs, rhymes, and games which tell about their occupations.

Classroom Preparation:

- Review the songs, fingerplays, rhymes, and games for each career.

Songs and Fingerplays:
- *When I Grow Up*
- *One Is For The Rocket*
- *The Wheels On The Bus*
- *The Firefighters*
- *Five Little Police Officers*
- *ABC Song*
- *Mr. Alligator*

Costumes:

- Give the children a choice of how to portray their occupations.
  - Let the children paint pictures of what they would like to be.
  - Pre-cut body masks for the children out of cardboard about 2½ feet long and 1½ feet wide. Cut holes in each one for the children's faces and arms. Let the children add features with collage materials.
  - Help the children make headbands to represent their occupations.

Nametags: Firefighter Hats

Decorations: Children's art

137

Set-up:

- Arrange the children's mats in the presentation area.

- Set out stools for children to sit on while being introduced.

- Get a copy of 'Floating Cloud' on the album *Playtime Parachute Fun* (Kimbo) for scarf dancing.

- Have the box of scarves nearby for scarf dancing.

- Have several balls nearby for the jugglers to use.

- Get a copy of 'Play Your Instruments and Make a Pretty Sound,' by Ella Jenkins on her album *Play Your Instruments and Make a Pretty Sound* (Folkways). You'll need this for the Rhythm Band.

- Have the rhythm instruments nearby for the musicians to play.

Refreshments:

The Baker's Delight

You'll Need:
Raisin bread
Butter
Cream cheese

To Make: Cut the raisin bread in quarters. Spread butter or cream cheese on each piece. Put on plates. Cover tightly and refrigerate.

PRESENTATION

Children slowly march in wearing their body masks or headbands or carrying their paintings and go to their mats.

Teacher welcomes everyone to the end-of-the-year program.

NARRATOR: "As you might already know, the children of today have limitless possibilities of careers from which to choose. We have been studying many of them and have had fun pretending to work at different occupations. Today, we will get a glimpse into the future. The children have each decided what they would like to be when they grow up. They will now share their ideas with you."

WHEN I GROW UP
(tune: The Prettiest Girl)

(This may be sung as a total group or the teacher may sing the first part and the children echo or half of the children sing the first part and the others echo. As a child's occupation is named, he steps forward for everyone to see.)

When I grow up .... (echo, "When I grow up")
I want to be .... (echo, "I want to be")
An astronaut .... (echo, 'An astronaut")
Just wait and see .... (echo, "Just wait and see")

Continue for each of the children.

NARRATOR: "(Child's name) has chosen the space age career as an astronaut." (That child comes forward and leads the rhyme.)

ONE IS FOR THE ROCKET

One is for the rocket standing straight and tall.
Two is for the stages, count them as they fall.
Three is for the cameras, watching earth below.
Four is for the weightlessness, which makes us float so slow.
Five is for the astronauts ready for the trip.
Six is for the space food packaged not to tip.
Seven is for the telescopes to study a far off star.
Eight is for the satellites, to be launched from afar.
Nine is for the instruments to help the research team.
Ten is for the countdown, ready to begin.
10, 9, 8, 7, 6, 5, 4, 3, 2, 1, 0 BLAST OFF!

by Susan Spaete

NARRATOR: "(Child's name) thinks that driving a bus is just the thing." (That child comes forward and leads the song.)

WHEELS ON THE BUS

The wheels on the bus go 'round and 'round,
'Round and 'round, 'round and 'round.
The wheels on the bus go 'round and 'round,
All through the town. (Roll arms)

The driver on the bus says, "Move on back,
Move on back, move on back."
The driver on the bus says, "Move on back,"
All through the town. (Motion back with hand)

The wipers on the bus go swish, swish, swish,
Swish, swish, swish, swish, swish, swish.
The wipers on the bus go swish, swish, swish,
All through the town. (Move arms back and forth)

The children on the bus go bumpity-bump,
Bumpity-bump, bumpity-bump.
The children on the bus go bumpity-bump,
All through the town. (Children move up and down)

The babies on the bus go 'Waa, waa, waa,
Waa, waa, waa, waa, waa, waa."
The babies on the bus go "Waa, waa, waa,"
All through the town. (Pretend to be rubbing eyes)

The mothers on the bus go, "Shhh, shhh, shhh,
Shhh, shhh, shhh, shhh, shhh, shhh."
The mothers on the bus go, "Shhh, shhh, shhh,"
All through the town. (Hold finger to lips)

The fathers on the bus say, "Look at that!
Look at that, look at that!"
The fathers on the bus say, "Look at that!"
All through the town. (Point to objects in room)

NARRATOR: "Dancing for a living is what (child's name) would like to do. (That child comes forward and passes out the scarves for scarf dancing. All of the children dance with their scarves while the music is playing. Afterwards they sit on their mats and the child collects the scarves.)

NARRATOR: "Driving a firetruck is what (child's name) would like to do." (That child comes forward and leads the fingerplay.)

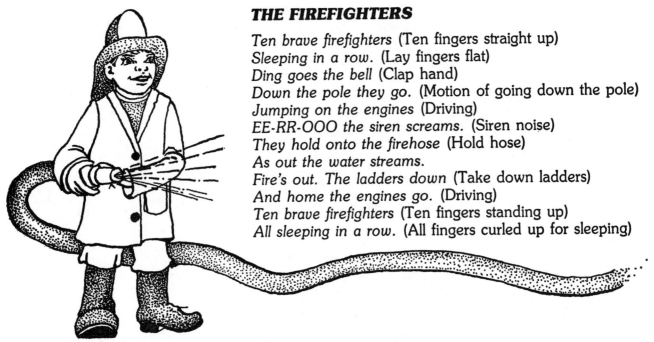

THE FIREFIGHTERS

Ten brave firefighters (Ten fingers straight up)
Sleeping in a row. (Lay fingers flat)
Ding goes the bell (Clap hand)
Down the pole they go. (Motion of going down the pole)
Jumping on the engines (Driving)
EE-RR-OOO the siren screams. (Siren noise)
They hold onto the firehose (Hold hose)
As out the water streams.
Fire's out. The ladders down (Take down ladders)
And home the engines go. (Driving)
Ten brave firefighters (Ten fingers standing up)
All sleeping in a row. (All fingers curled up for sleeping)

NARRATOR: "(Child's name) has so much fun with balls and would like to be a juggler. Watch as we conduct juggling practice." (Pass out the balls to the children who want to be jugglers.) Have the children:
— Bounce the balls in front of them.
— Bounce the balls back and forth with friends.
— Toss the balls in the air and catch them.
(Collect the balls.)

NARRATOR: "(Child's name) likes music and would like to be a musician." (Have the children come forward. Hand out the instruments to the children who would like to be musicians or to all of the children. The children can play their instruments along with the record 'Play Your Instruments and Make a Pretty Sound.' Collect the instruments.)

NARRATOR: "A police officer is what (child's name) has decided to be." (Have this child come forward and lead the fingerplay.)

FIVE LITTLE POLICE OFFICERS

Five strong police, standing by a store.
One became a traffic cop and then there were four.
Four strong police watching over me.
One took home a lost child, then there were three.
Three strong police dressed all in blue,
One stopped a speeding car, then there were two.
Two strong police, how fast they can run,
One caught a thief, now there is one.
One strong police saw some smoke one day.
He called the firefighters, who came right away.

140

NARRATOR: "(Child's name) wants to be a teacher." (Have this child come forward, lead the song and then lead the audience in singing it again.)

ABC SONG

A B C D E F G H I J K L M N O P Q R S T U V W X Y Z.
Now I've said my A B C's. Next time won't you sing with me

NARRATOR: "Working with exotic animals at the zoo is what (child's name) would do as a zookeeper." (Have the child come forward and lead the others in Mr. Alligator.)

MR. ALLIGATOR

Five little monkeys swinging from the tree, (Wave five fingers)
Teasing Mr. Alligator, "Can't catch me, can't catch me."
Along came Mr. Alligator quietly as can be. (Make swimming motion)
Snap! (Clap)

Four little monkeys swinging from the tree, (Wave four fingers)
Teasing Mr. Alligator, "Can't catch me, can't catch me."
Along came Mr. Alligator quietly as can be.
Snap! (Clap)

Three little monkeys swinging from the tree. (Wave three fingers)
Teasing Mr. Alligator, "Can't catch me, can't catch me."
Along came Mr. Alligator quietly as can be.
Snap! (Clap)

Two little monkeys swinging from the tree, (Wave two fingers)
Teasing Mr. Alligator, "Can't catch me, can't catch me."
Along came Mr. Alligator quietly as can be.
Snap! (Clap)

One little monkey swinging from the tree, (Wave one finger)
Teasing Mr. Alligator, "Can't catch me, can't catch me."
Along came Mr. Alligator quietly as can be.
Snap! (Clap)

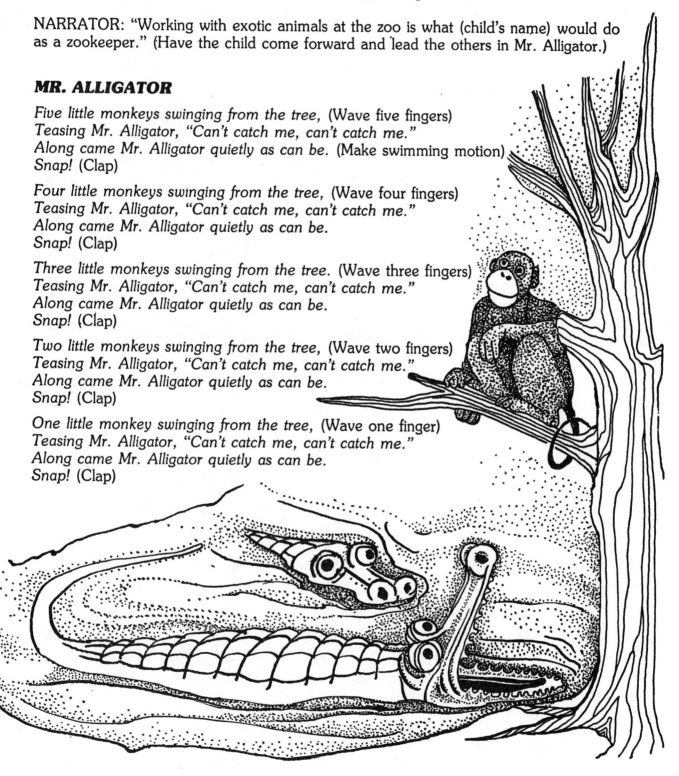

NARRATOR: "Thank you for joining us today as we looked into the future. Please join us now for refreshments."

TEDDY BEARS PICNIC

Children Enter	Walking in Holding Their Bears
Teacher	Welcome
Children	Introductions
Fingerplay	*Five Little Teddy Bears*
Song	*The Bear Went Over the Mountain*
Activity	*Teddy Bear, Teddy Bear Turn Around*
Fingerplay	*Honey Bears*
Drama	The Three Bears
Dance	*Dance of the Dancing Bears*
Guest	Smokey T. Bear
Refreshments	Picnic

Program Covers — Fold construction paper in half and have the children glue teddy bear faces to the covers. Create the faces by cutting five inch circles from colored paper and then gluing construction paper ears and facial features to each one.

PREPARATION

Children's Planning:

- Talk with the children about all of the fun they have had throughout the year.

- Tell the children that they're going to have an end-of-the-year picnic with their families and teddy bears. Ask the children what foods they like to have on picnics. Play "If I were going on a picnic I'd like to eat ＿＿＿＿＿＿ ." Write down their suggestions.

- Talk about games the children might like to play at a picnic, such as 'Keep Balloons in the Air' or 'Find the Pennies in the Grass.' Use their suggestions at your picnic.

- Read the story of *The Three Bears*.

Classroom Preparation:

- Review the songs and rhymes with the children.

- Listen to the Spanish Dance, 'Chocolate' from Tchaikowsky's *Nutcracker Suite*. As the children are listening, they can free dance to the rhythm.

Songs and Fingerplays:

- *Five Little Teddy Bears*
- *The Bear Went Over the Mountain*
- *Teddy Bear, Teddy Bear Turn Around*
- *Honey Bears*

Costumes: None

Nametags: Teddy Bears

Decorations:

- Let the children choose what artwork they would like to display for the picnic.

- Have large teddy bears sitting around the room, posters hanging on the walls, and small teddy bears sitting on the refreshment table.

PRESENTATION

Children holding their bears walk in to the music of 'Teddy Bear's Picnic.' They sit down on their mats.

Teacher welcomes everyone to the end-of-the-year picnic and reviews a few highlights which occurred during the year.

NARRATOR: "Bears are popular with all ages. Today we would like you to meet some very special bears." (Have children stand and introduce themselves along with their bears. For example, "I'm Josh and this is my bear 'Fuzzy'." They should remain standing.)

NARRATOR: "The children and their bears would like to tell you about five bears they know."

Set-up:

- Contact an adult to play Smokey T. Bear to talk with the children about summer safety. Perhaps your community has a public safety officer or a police officer who can talk with the children.
- You'll need a copy of the song 'Teddy Bears Picnic' from the album *Anne Margaret Sings For The Sesame Street Generations*, Balmur Ltd.
- Make 'Winner Badges' for each child for the great year they've all had together.
- Have the children's mats on the floor for them to sit on.
- Blow up balloons for 'Keep Balloons in the Air.'
- Collect pennies for 'Find the Pennies in the Grass.'
- Gather needed materials for other games the children suggested playing.
- If you're going to tell the story of 'The Three Bears,' make the felt characters or practice pantomiming the story with the children.

Refreshments: Notes should be sent home several weeks before the program telling the parents about the end-of-the-year picnic. It should include information about the picnic. (You could have a potluck picnic with each family bringing a dish to pass or have each family bring its own picnic food and the school provide the drinks.) Remind them that their children should bring teddy bears with them to the program. They should put an ID tag on each bear, telling its name, owner's name, and telephone number.

FIVE LITTLE TEDDY BEARS

Five little teddy bears were getting ready to play,
The first one said, "Have a happy day."
The second one said, "Let's have some honey."
The third one said, "Isn't he funny."
The fourth one said, "Read a book to me."
The fifth one said, "Oh, let me see!"
When they all were tired and the book was read,
Five little teddy bears tumbled into bed.

NARRATOR: "Some bears are very adventuresome. Listen as the children tell you about a bear who went exploring over the mountain."

THE BEAR WENT OVER THE MOUNTAIN

The bear went over the mountain,
The bear went over the mountain,
The bear went over the mountain,
To see what he could see.
To see what he could see.
To see what he could see.
The other side of the mountain,
The other side of the mountain,
The other side of the mountain,
Was all that he could see.
Was all that he could see.
Was all that he could see.
The other side of the mountain
Was all that he could see.

NARRATOR: "Like people, bears need their exercise. Watch as the bears workout."

TEDDY BEAR, TEDDY BEAR TURN AROUND

Teddy bear, teddy bear turn around,
Teddy bear, teddy bear touch the ground,
Teddy bear, teddy bear read the news,
Teddy bear, teddy bear tie your shoes,
Teddy bear, teddy bear go upstairs,
Teddy bear, teddy bear say your prayers,
Teddy bear, teddy bear turn out the light,
Teddy bear, teddy bear say good night . . .
"GOOD NIGHT!"

NARRATOR: "Bears have a favorite food. Can you guess what it is? Listen to the children."

HONEY BEARS

A little brown bear went searching for honey.
Isn't it funny, a bear wanting honey?
He sniffed in the breeze. (Sniff)
And he listened for bees. (Hold hand to ear)
And would you believe, he even climbed trees.
(One fist on top of the other)

NARRATOR: (If you are not able to have a picnic, present the story of 'The Three Bears.' Have the children act out the story as the narrator tells it or use the felt board to tell the story.)

NARRATOR: "Now our bears would like to dance around the stage for you." (The children and their bears free dance to 'Chocolate.')

NARRATOR: "And now a special guest . . . that famous bear, SMOKEY!" (Smokey appears, says a few words about summer safety to the children and then distributes 'Winner Badges' to all of them for the great year they have had.)

Refreshments: Invite all of the families along with Smokey T. Bear to the picnic area. Enjoy each others company while eating. Afterwards play several games if you have time.

BUILDING BLOCKS

Felt Board Fun

by Liz and Dick Wilmes. Make your felt board come alive. Discover how versatile it is as the children become involved with a wide range of activities. This unique book has over 150 ideas with accompanying patterns.
ISBN 0-943452-02-3 $14.95

Parachute Play

by Liz and Dick Wilmes. A year 'round approach to one of the most versatile pieces of large muscle equipment. Starting with basic techniques, PARACHUTE PLAY provides over 100 activities to use with your parachute.
ISBN 0-943452-03-1 $ 7.95

Exploring Art

by Liz and Dick Wilmes. EXPLORING ART is divided by months. Over 250 art ideas for paint, chalk, doughs, scissors, and more. Easy to set-up in your classroom.
ISBN 0-943452-05-8 $16.95

Everyday Bulletin Boards

by Wilmes and Moehling. Features borders, murals, backgrounds, and other open-ended art to display on your bulletin board. Plus board ideas with patterns, which teachers can make and use to enhance their curriculum.
ISBN 0-943452-09-0 $ 8.95

Gifts, Cards, and Wraps

by Wilmes and Zavodsky. Help the children sparkle with the excitement of gift-giving. Filled with thoughtful gifts, unique wraps, and special cards which the children can make and give. They're sure to bring smiles.
ISBN 0-943452-06-6 $ 7.95

Imagination Stretchers

by Liz and Dick Wilmes. Perfect for whole language. Over 400 conversation starters for creative discussions, simple lists, and beginning dictation and writing.
ISBN 0-943452-04-X $ 6.95

Parent Programs and Open Houses

by Susan Spaete. Filled with a wide variety of year 'round presentations, pre-registration ideas, open houses, and end-of-the-year gatherings. All involve the children from the planning stages through the programs.
ISBN 0-943452-08-2 $ 9.95

Classroom Parties.

by Susan Spaete. Each party plan suggests decorations, trimmings, and snacks which the children can easily make to set a festive mood. Choose from games, songs, art activities, stories, and related experiences which will add to the spirit and fun.
ISBN 0-943452-07-4 $ 8.95

The Circle Time Series

by Liz and Dick Wilmes. Hundreds of activities for large and small groups of children. Each one is filled with Language and Active games, Fingerplays, Songs, Stories, Snacks, and more. A great resource for every library shelf.

Circle Time Book

Captures the spirit of 39 holidays and seasons.
ISBN 0-943452-00-7   **$9.95**

Everyday Circle Times

Over 900 ideas. Choose from 48 topics divided into 7 sections: self concept, basic concepts, animals, foods, science, occupations, and recreation.
ISBN 0-943452-01-5   **$14.95**

Yearful of Circle Times

52 different topics to use weekly, by seasons, or mixed throughout the year. New Friends, Signs of Fall, Snowman Fun, and much more.
ISBN 0-943452-10-4   **$14.95**

More Everyday Circle Times

Divided into the same 7 sections as EVERYDAY. Features new topics such as Birds and Pizza, plus all new ideas for some familiar topics contained in EVERYDAY.
ISBN 0-943452-14-7   **$14.95**

Learning Centers

by Liz and Dick Wilmes. Hundreds of open-ended activities to quickly involve and excite your children. You'll use it every time you plan and whenever you need a quick, additional activity. A must for every teacher's bookshelf.
ISBN 0-943452-13-9   **$16.95**

Make-Take Games

by Liz and Dick Wilmes. Features 32 large, colorful games which are easy to make. Children will have fun everyday playing them by themselves or in groups.
ISBN 0-943452-11-2   **$12.95**

Companion Pattern Set

Game-making made even easier! Set of 21 posterboard size sheets to accompany MAKE-TAKE GAMES. Ready-to-use, a great time saver. Plus use the patterns for other activities which need a visual aid.
ISBN 0-943452-12-0   **$24.95**

Large 22"x28" Sheets